Merton
EXHIBITION

THOMAS MERTON
The Poet and the Contemplative Life

■

An Exhibition
Compiled by Patrick T. Lawlor
Foreword by Kenneth A. Lohf

New York: Columbia University Libraries, 1990

Copyright 1990
The Trustees of Columbia University
in the City of New York

ISBN 0-9607862-2-8

Cover: *Merton in a study hut at Gethsemani, early 1960s.*
Frontispiece: *Photograph by Edward Rice of Merton at the Abbey of Gethsemani, 1949.*

Contents

Foreword *7*
Introduction *9*
The Catalogue:
   The Secular Life: 1915 – 1941 . . . . *13*
   The Novitiate: 1942 – 1949 . . . . *20*
   The Monk and Teacher: 1950 – 1958 . . . . *28*
   The Public Years: 1959 – 1964 . . . . *39*
   The Hermitage Years: 1965 – 1968 . . . . *50*
   The Legacy: 1968 – 1988 . . . . *56*
Index *61*

Foreword

*F*raternity brother, member of the track team, an editor of the *Yearbook* and the *Jester*, Thomas Merton, in his three-piece suit with gold watch chain, looked more like a businessman than an undergraduate when he attended Columbia College and the Graduate School from 1935 to 1939. The friends he made during his college years, notably Robert Lax and Robert Giroux, and his mentor at the University, Professor Mark Van Doren, were to remain his friends for life. The file of correspondence that Professor Van Doren received from Merton, comprising some seventy-five lengthy and revealing letters enclosing ninety-five manuscripts of poems, was presented by Professor Van Doren to the Rare Book and Manuscript Library in September 1969, the year following Merton's death. This important group of documents became the basis for the Library's extensive holdings and is the prime resource for the study of the life, thought, and writings of the well-known poet, priest, and public figure.

After he entered the Trappist monastery of Gethsemani in Kentucky in 1941, Merton began another of his long-time friendships and correspondences, that with Sister Thérèse Lentfoehr. She wrote to him frequently on birthdays, holidays, and special occasions, and he responded by sending her long replies and drafts of poems and selections from his journals. He also sent Sister Thérèse a copy of the typewritten manuscript of *The Seven Storey Mountain*, his best-selling autobiography recounting his life through his early years as a Trappist monk that brought him widespread fame. Sister Thérèse's extensive Merton collection of letters, manuscripts, drawings, photographs, and inscribed first editions, including the manuscript of *The Seven Storey Mountain*, was acquired in 1988, and this remarkably personal and far-reaching archive, along with the Mark Van Doren correspondence and manuscripts, forms the foundation for the current exhibition.

At commencement exercises in June 1961 Merton was awarded *in absentia* the University Medal for Excellence at the urging of Professor Van Doren. In thanking President Grayson Kirk for the award, Merton acknowledged "very heartily the love which I have never ceased to have for Columbia and which has grown with the years." Merton responded to the honor by presenting to the University a copy of his book *The Ox Mountain Parable of Meng Tzu*, privately printed by Victor Hammer at the Stamperia del Santuccio in Lexington, Kentucky. This was the first of Merton's many gifts to the Rare Book and Manuscript Library, which, over the next seven years until his death, came to total more than 120 manuscripts and typescripts of poems and meditations, as well as thirty-seven editions of his writings, many of them fragile pamphlets issued in small printings.

An extensive collection of Merton's correspondence was also received from his literary agent, Curtis Brown, and further smaller but important groups of letters were presented over the years by Robert Lax, Random House, and Robert Shepherd. Preserved now at the Library is a major Thomas Merton archive comprising the papers of his mentor and teacher, several of his closest friends, and his literary agent. This collection of original documents will continue to provide the Merton student and scholar with a resource that permits the study of his unusual combination of careers and talents as author and poet, as apologist for his understanding of religious faith, and as a concerned and responsible individual conscience in the twentieth century.

Inscribed first editions, autograph letters and manuscripts, photographs, and drawings selected from the notable gifts described above are included in this anniversary exhibition held in the Rare Book and Manuscript Library's Kempner Exhibition Room from December 7, 1989, to February 23, 1990. The 177 rare items, chosen to depict the significant events in Merton's literary and religious careers, are described in detail in the illustrated catalogue that accompanies the exhibition.

>   Kenneth A. Lohf
>   Librarian for Rare Books
>   and Manuscripts

Introduction

The name of Thomas Merton has achieved an almost mythical status. This is unfortunate but predictable due to the nature of his life and the events surrounding his death. Merton was born in Padres, France, on January 31, 1915. His parents, Owen and Ruth, were both artists. Raised in France, the United States, and England, Merton lost his mother when he was six years old and his father when he was fifteen. From an early age Merton was aware of death, and his travels left him without any real sense of home. At Cambridge his energy and intelligence were directed towards deriving as much enjoyment out of life as he could. His guardian, Tom Bennett, advised him to continue his studies in the United States, and this Merton did with success at Columbia College, where he impressed Mark Van Doren and made a number of friendships which were to last the rest of his life. Merton's restless spirit drove him to question the values of the life he was leading. It is this pursuit of truth and value which characterizes Merton's life and makes his writings so challenging.

After living a fast-paced life at Columbia and with prospects of a promising intellectual and artistic career, Merton turned his back on the secular world and entered the Cistercian Monastery of Our Lady of Gethsemani in rural Kentucky on December 10, 1941. For the next seven years he studied for the priesthood in the demanding physical conditions characteristic of monasteries of the Cistercian Order of the Strict Observance. A born writer, Merton continued to write in the monastery and on October 4, 1948, Harcourt, Brace published his autobiography, *The Seven Storey Mountain*. Literally overnight Merton went from being a little-known Trappist poet to an internationally celebrated author. Merton's story of a worldly young man who has the integrity and courage to reject all that the world has to offer in order to attain spiritual peace clearly struck a chord in postwar America. Also, the detailed account of life in a Cistercian monastery revealed a fascinating medieval world unknown to many. However, the conflict between the artistic and religious aspects of his life was a paradox which he was was never able to resolve.

Merton remained in the abbey of Gethsemani till 1968, producing numerous books of poetry, essays, and spiritual guides. With the election of a new abbot, Merton was allowed more freedom to travel, and in September of that year he left Gethsemani to attend a conference of Benedictine abbots in Bangkok. He died there at the age of fifty-three after being electrocuted by a standing fan which had an exposed wire.

The date was December 10, 1968, exactly twenty-seven years to the day after he had entered the Cistercian Order. Throughout his years in the monastery, Merton had extended his spiritual and social concerns, becoming a leading voice in the disarmament and social justice movements, as well as a bridge between Eastern and Western religious traditions. His writings had earned him a reputation as a man of vision and truth, a deeply spiritual man capable of giving voice to the inarticulate desires of the human soul.

Note: Unless otherwise specified, all quotations in the text are from *The Seven Storey Mountain*.

The Catalogue

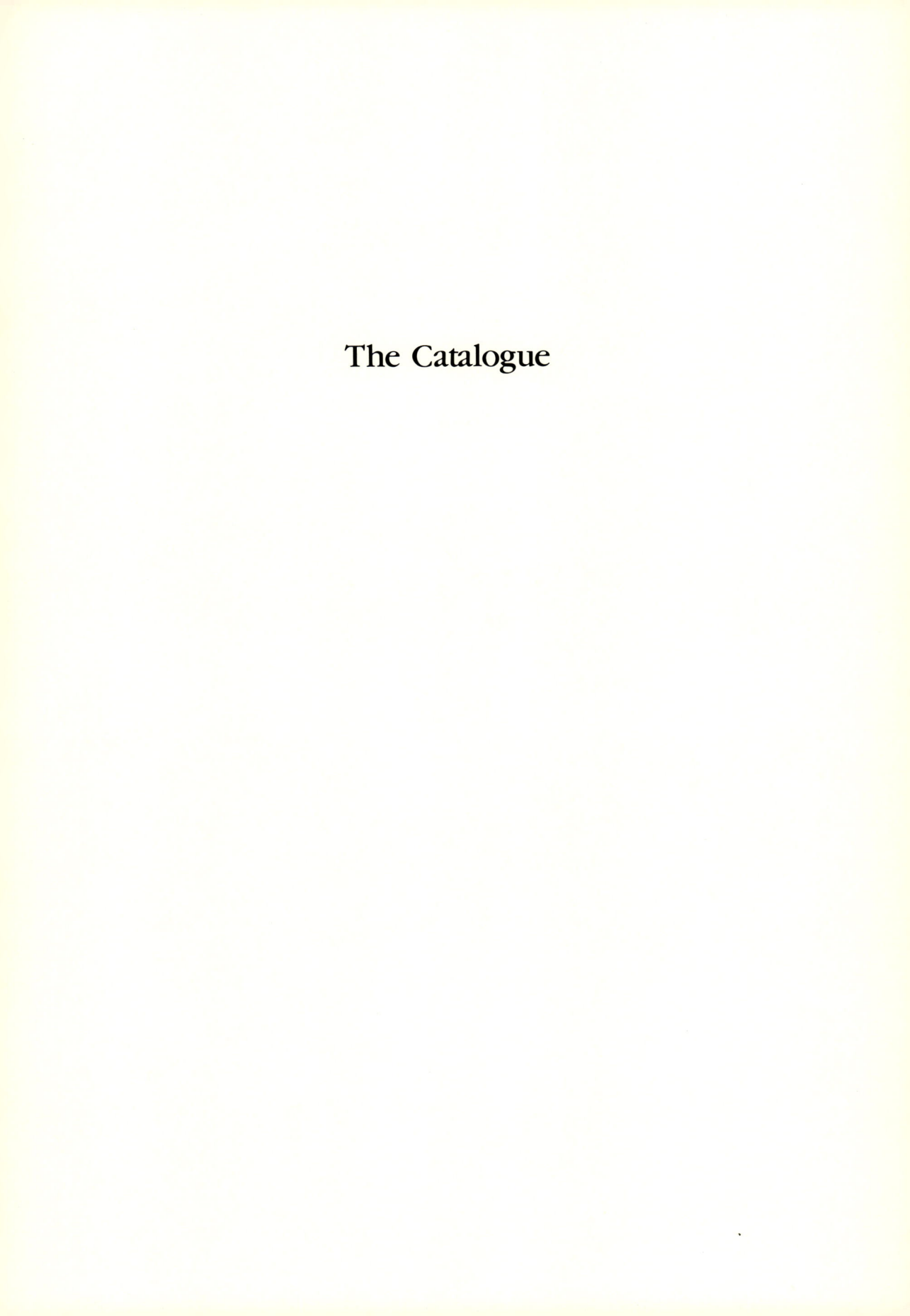

The Secular Life: 1915 – 1941

*T*he period of Merton's life up to his entry into the monastery of Gethsemani is fully detailed in *The Seven Storey Mountain* and in his *Secular Journal*. The first half of Merton's life was full of change, instability, and death. The loss of his father and mother combined with regular family moves gave Merton a restless nature. When he arrived at Columbia he was more worldly and well-traveled than any of his contemporaries and soon became something of a campus star. His active life — art editor of the *Jester*, editor of the Columbia *Yearbook*, runner for the cross-country team, and member of the Alpha Delta Phi fraternity — led to lasting friendships with Robert Lax, Edward Rice, Robert Gibney, Robert Gerdy, Daniel Walsh, and Seymour Freedgood. Baptized into the Roman Catholic faith a year after graduating from Columbia, Merton continued his graduate studies but felt an increasing pull towards the Church. After being turned down by the Franciscans in June 1940, Merton made a retreat during Easter 1941 at the Cistercian Monastery of Our Lady of Gethsemani in Kentucky. This experience profoundly moved him and without informing anyone of his plans, Merton entered the monastery on December 10, 1941, having first destroyed some of the manuscripts of his novels and sending the rest of his journals and poems to his friend and mentor Mark Van Doren.

- Photograph of Owen Merton (1887–1931).

- Photograph of Ruth Merton (1887–1921).

- Photograph of Ruth Merton with her children Thomas and John Paul [ca. 1920].

- Owen Merton. Watercolor of a street scene in Bermuda. Signed and dated 1922. 8×9.5 inches.

    In *The Seven Storey Mountain* Merton fondly recalls his father's artistic ability: "My father painted like Cézanne and understood the southern French landscape the way Cézanne did. His vision of the world was sane, full of balance, full of veneration for structure, for the relation of masses and for the circumstances that impress an individual identity on each created thing."

- Owen Merton. Watercolor of a hillside and flank of a cathedral. Signed and dated 1923. 14×19 inches.

- Owen Merton. Watercolor of the village of St. Antonin. Signed and dated 1927. 14 × 18 inches.

    In 1925 Owen Merton moved with Thomas to the southern French town of St. Antonin. "Here in this amazing, ancient town, the very pattern of the place, of the houses and streets and of nature itself, the circling hills, the cliffs and trees, all focused my attention upon the one important central fact of the church and what it contained."

- Photograph of Merton with his fraternity at Columbia College [1935].

    In 1935, his first year at Columbia, Merton pledged Alpha Delta Phi fraternity. In this photograph he is seated in the second row, third from right.

- *The Columbian: 1937.* New York: Columbia University, 1937.

    Merton's picture appeared throughout the 1937 *Yearbook,* fourteen times in fact, much to his later disgust.

- Photograph of Merton, Robert Lax, and Ralph de Toledano in the office of the *Jester*, 1937.

    At the end of the 1936 school year, Merton was elected art editor of the *Jester* as well as editor of the Columbia *Yearbook.*

- *The Columbia Jester*, Vol. XXXVII, No. 1, 1937. New York: Columbia University.

    As art editor of the *Jester* Merton designed this humorous cover depicting the typical Columbia College year.

- Photograph of Merton at Columbia College [1937].

    The official class photograph of Merton. "They did not have to be very acute to see through the dumb, self-satisfied expression in all those portraits in the Columbia University *Yearbook* of 1937."

- Edward Rice. Photograph of Merton in the Columbia College quadrangle [ca. 1937].

- "Nature and Art in William Blake." Typewritten manuscript, 103 p. 1939.

    Merton's master's essay. "I did not realize how providential a subject it actually was! What it amounted to, was a study of Blake's reaction against every kind of literalism and naturalism, classical realism in art, because of his own ideal which was essentially mystical and supernatural."

- Photograph of Merton's apartment (second floor with balcony) at 35 Perry Street.

    Shortly after receiving his master's degree from Columbia, Merton moved into this apartment in Greenwich Village.

- Thomas Merton. Photograph of Edward Rice and Robert Lax, 1939.

    During the summer of 1939, Merton, Lax, and Rice stayed at the Marcus cottage in Olean, New York, owned by Lax's brother-in-law. They all planned to write novels;

Left to right: Merton, Robert Lax, and Ralph de Toledano in the office of the Jester, *1937.*

Merton's was entitled "The Straits of Dover," then "The Night Before the Battle," and finally "The Labyrinth."

■ Edward Rice. Photograph of Merton in Olean, New York, 1939.

■ Edward Rice. Photograph of Merton and Robert Lax on the porch of the Marcus cottage in Olean, New York, 1939.

■ Autograph letter signed, to Mark Van Doren, 1 p. New York, March 30, 1939.
After Van Doren had written to him using the language of *Finnegans Wake,* Merton responded in kind. In this delightful letter, Merton displays to his teacher, "Mr ffin Dornian," his mastery of Joycean language and wit.

■ Autograph letter signed, to Mark Van Doren, 8 p. New York, August 18, 1939.
The hopes and frustrations of a young writer come through in this revealing letter.

Merton informs Van Doren that he has just finished a novel ("160,000 words. Weighs five and a half pounds"). Entitled "The Night Before the Battle," it is an "intellectual autobiography" covering the years 1929 to 1939. He tells Van Doren that Farrar & Rinehart are considering it, and also that he has taken Van Doren's advice and kept away from the "private language of Lax's and my *Jester* and so on." He goes on to list the various literary rejections of the summer and adds "I think it is about time somebody took *something* of mine, & I hope it will be the novel!"

- Autograph notebook, 62 p. [1939–1944].

    The first pages of this notebook contain notes on philosophy and Jacobean plays, written before his entry into Gethsemani. Most of the entries are related to his study of philosophers and theologians. First Merton copies out texts from each of the authors, often dates each entry, and then supplies his own interpretation or explanation. Shown is a page of notes on Jean Buridan and Aristotle with an interesting drawing of the head of an angel at the top of the page containing the notes on Aristotle.

- "A Signed Confession of Crimes Against the State." Typewritten manuscript, with autograph corrections and additions, 1 p. 1939.

    This mock confession shows Merton's hostility towards the State. His act of confession becomes a statement of freedom. In confessing to living, to enjoying nature, to the sun shining, Merton declares his commitment to the individual and his contempt for the machinery of the bureaucratic state.

- Typewritten letter signed, to Mark Van Doren, 1 p. Olean, New York, August 25, 1940.

    Having been rejected by the Franciscans, Merton spent the summer with Robert Lax at the Marcus cottage in Olean, New York, writing a novel and generally enjoying himself. Hiding his bitter disappointment from Van Doren, Merton discusses his plans to get a job teaching at a Catholic college — "a place to eat and sleep and a typewriter to write on and a couple of classes to talk in and whatever money they can spare for the movies, and not much talk of seething ambition." Eventually, Merton got a job teaching English at St. Bonaventure College and became a Franciscan Tertiary (a lay member living in society).

- Series of pen and ink drawings entitled "Army Conversation" [1940–1941].

- Pen and ink drawing entitled "The Footrace" [1940–1941].

    Men and women with beards was a trademark of Merton's humorous drawings.

- Calligraphic pen and ink drawings entitled "Patriotic Singer" and "Drunk Danse [sic]" [1940–1941].

- Pen and ink calligraphic drawing of the Angel of Annunciation [1941].

    This figure, composed of the "Hail Mary," has the plea "Pray for T.M." as part of its composition.

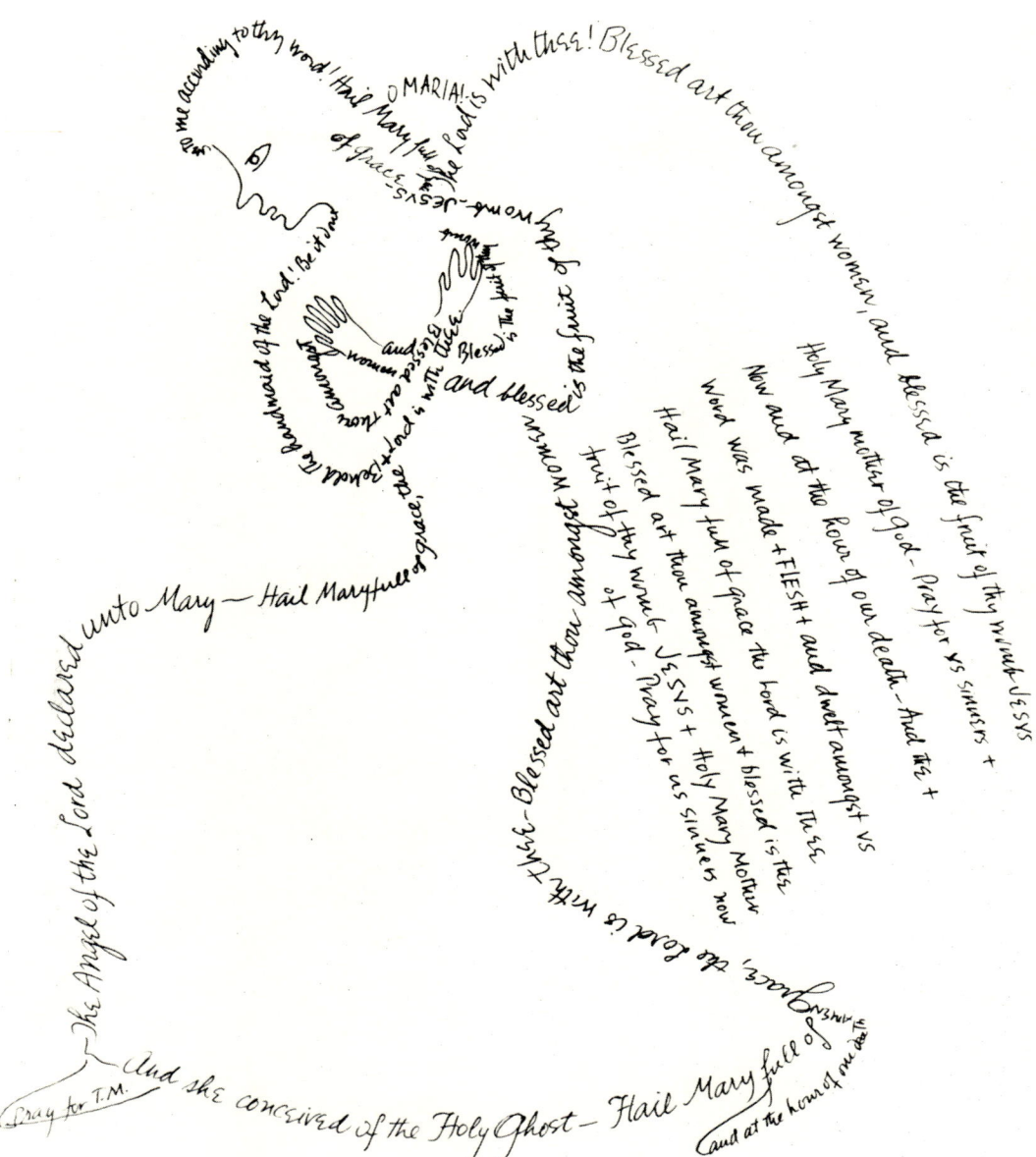

Pen and ink calligraphic drawing by Merton of the Angel of the Annunciation, ca. 1941.

■ "The Journal of My Escape from the Nazis." Typewritten manuscript, with autograph corrections, 62 p. [1941].

This early version of *My Argument with the Gestapo* contains an interesting prologue by Merton in which he considers the state of the modern novel. "The novel is a dead medium" opens this version of Merton's only published novel.

- *My Argument with the Gestapo.* New York: Doubleday, 1969.

    Although Merton was in the United States at the time of the London Blitz, he chose to set this novel in war-torn London and Paris. He wrote this novel in 1941, but it was rejected by a number of publishers at the time. Merton tries to understand and explore the nature of such a devastating war and finds only moral and spiritual decay on both sides. There is much satire and wordplay in the book: "It was the kind of book I liked to write, full of double-talk and all kinds of fancy ideas that sounded like Franz Kafka."

- Typewritten letter signed, to Mark Van Doren, 1 p. St. Bonaventure College, New York, December 9, 1941.

    Merton made a retreat to the Cistercian Monastery of Gethsemani in Kentucky in April 1941. This visit decided the course of his life until his accidental death in 1968. On the eve of his departure for Gethsemani, Merton sent copies of his poems and journals, as well as the only manuscript he valued, "Journal of My Escape from the Nazis," to Mark Van Doren. In this letter Merton mentions nothing of his decision to Van Doren, only that he is in a hurry and that he will explain more in the near future.

- Autograph letter signed, to Mark Van Doren, 2 p. Trappist, Kentucky, [December 13] 1941.

    Informing Van Doren that he has been tentatively accepted at the monastery, Merton makes a gift of the manuscript of "Journal of My Escape from the Nazis" to Van Doren. Merton expresses his joy in having found a place of renewal and salvation in his poem "Letter to My Friends": "Here are your ruins all rebuilt as fast as you destroyed them." Although the tone is a bit shrill, the poem clearly expresses Merton's eager commitment to his new life.

- Photograph of Merton with fellow members of the faculty of St. Bonaventure College on commencement day, 1941.

    Merton was on the staff of St. Bonaventure from the fall of 1940 until he entered the Abbey of Gethsemani on December 10, 1941.

- "My reasons for asking exemption from combat duty in the army, under Selective Service law of 1940." Typewritten manuscript, with autograph corrections, 3 p. [1941].

    In March of 1941 Merton received a notice from the Draft Board. In response, Merton sent a letter explaining his wish to be considered a partial conscientious objector. However, after his medical examination Merton was classified 1-B due to the poor state of his teeth. In December he was sent a notice of a second examination. When he found out that he would likely be re-classified 1-A, he expedited his planned entry into the Cistercian Order.

Page from the typewritten prologue of "Journal of My Escape from the Nazis," 1941.

Lyly's Euphues is not really a novel, (nor do I particularly like it either,) But it reminds me of Castiglione's Courtier, which is even less a novel, yet is a sort of a novel too and a good one if you take the word novel in its widest sense. It has something that might pass today for a novel's structure.

But my favorite novels are all journals, encyclopaedic journals, containing everything one man is interested in, everything one man has ever seen in the world. For me the word novel has no longer any precise meaning. It simply means a long book in prose that does not deal with some technical subject, and is not a textbook but a book written for the delight of the intellect.

I say for the delight of the intellect, and not primarily for the salvation of the soul, because the value of the novel is an intellectual rather than a moral one, primarily. A novel is good when it is true: true to two things, to itself and to the order in life itself. It must be true to life, but in the widest sense: it must be true to what is, universally, but it doesn't have to be true to your life, you who live in a cupboard somewhere on Sixth avenue, you who live on the upper west side of New York, you who live in Larchmont. It merely has to be true. But if it is true, and shows the true order in things, then a moral order must also be implicit in it somewhere, but that does not necessarily have to come out in a sermon.

If a novel preaches no sermon at all, it suffices that it be true, implicitly, to the moral order in the universe.

The Novitiate: 1942–1949

On February 21, 1942, Thomas Merton received his novice's habit and became Brother M. Louis Merton, O.S.C.O. For the next few years Merton studied, prayed, did hard manual labor, and wrote. On March 19, 1944, Merton took Simple Vows signifying temporary profession as a monk. In November of the same year, New Directions published Merton's first book of poems, *Thirty Poems,* edited and selected by Mark Van Doren. This was followed in 1946 by a second volume of poems entitled *A Man in the Divided Sea.* On March 19, 1947, Merton was consecrated a monk after making his solemn profession. In 1948 six books by Thomas Merton were published, one of which, *The Seven Storey Mountain,* marked Thomas Merton's arrival as a writer of international prominence. The phenomenal success of *The Seven Storey Mountain* guaranteed future critical attention for any book by Thomas Merton. The popularity of his autobiography enabled Merton to open the minds of many people to the mysteries of religious vocation and experience. As he continued to grow in spiritual insight, his writings inspired and counseled a generation.

- Photographs of the Abbey of Gethsemani and its entrance, with its famous greeting "PAX INTRANTIBUS" (Peace to those who enter).

- Photograph of Merton as a monk [ca. 1941].
  When requested by his friend and fellow poet Sister Thérèse Lentfoehr to send a photograph, Merton sent this suitably anonymous picture of himself in the Cloister Garden at Gethsemani, informing her, "You can always use pictures of me as a secular."

- "Daily Schedule." Autograph manuscript, 1 p. [ca. 1942].
  Merton sent this schedule, which he had pasted on the wall of the vault where he worked, to Sister Thérèse Lentfoehr. His days as a cleric were full, but he would take time to pray alone in church whenever possible.

- "Novitiate Journal." Autograph manuscript, 14 p. 1941–1942.
  Merton kept two notebooks during his novitiate, both of which were destroyed except for these few pages. Interpersed with spiritual notes are seven poems: "A Letter to My Friends," "How Long We Wait," "Cana," "St. Paul," "Trappists Working,"

The Abbey of Our Lady of Gethsemani.

"The Ointment," and "The Candlemas Procession." Also shown is Merton's note to Sister Thérèse Lentfoehr regarding the fragments.

■ *Early Poems/1940–42.* Lexington: The Anvil Press, 1971.

These early poems reveal the degree to which the young Merton was disillusioned with society and fascinated by the creative use of language. T. S. Eliot and W. H. Auden clearly influenced both Merton's images and tone. The spiritual path seems to be the only way open to the poet who is lost in a world without direction and without hope. Although the intensity of some of the poems is unsettling, there are many memorable images and much wit in this collection of sixteen poems.

Albert Ulmann Fund

■ Autograph notebook, 62 p. 1939–1943.

This notebook contains a mixture of notes, poems, and translations, most of which were written after his entry into the monastery. There are notes on St. Augustine's *De Musica* and *City of God,* Aristotle's *De Memoria,* George Peele's *Old Wive's Tale* and *Arayngement of Paris,* Apollinaire's *Anecdotique,* Rilke, and Saint John of the Cross. Shown is Merton's moving poem on the death of his brother, John Paul, who was killed on active service in 1943 when his plane went down over the North Sea.

- "Hymn, of not much praise, for New York City." Typewritten manuscript, with autograph corrections, 2 p. [ca. 1940].

    In his early poetry Merton was much concerned with themes of alienation, loss, and confusion. This poem, published in *Thirty Poems,* uses the metaphor of a zoo ("this seasick zoo of buildings") for the living conditions in New York. As the poem progresses, the zoo turns into a prison/hospital in which the living and the dead cannot be distinguished.

- *Thirty Poems.* Norfolk: New Directions, 1944.

    Published on November 20, 1944, this was Merton's first published book, dedicated to the "Virgin Mary, the Queen of Poets." Mark Van Doren helped Merton select and arrange these carefully crafted lyric poems. The tone is one of a poet who is secure in his spiritual commitment within a natural setting. With echoes of T. S. Eliot, Merton places at a critical distance the restless world outside the monastery gates. Throughout, we see examples of Merton's love of the delicate phrase and arresting image — "rain / That lies in the windprints of rocks." His moving, almost transcendent elegy to his brother, John Paul, is one of the triumphs of Merton's poetical life.

    Gift of Diana Trilling

- Autograph letter signed, to Mark Van Doren, 2 p. Trappist, Kentucky, December 26, 1944.

    The publication of *Thirty Poems* clearly gave Merton much pleasure. In this letter he expresses his thanks to Van Doren for selecting the poems: "I live like a man on top of a mountain & it is easy for me to get off rhetorical questions like 'Why do people insist on fighting against God' but then I remember where I used to stand in the valley of the various shadows. . . ." In closing he mentions the various writing projects which he is working on for the monastery, as well as his own ideas for possible future publications.

- "April." Typewritten manuscript, with autograph corrections, 1 p. [1941].

    Of the composition of this poem, published in *A Man in the Divided Sea,* Merton writes: "And I, an Englishman,. . .went walking around the city, weaving in and out of the crowds, and thinking up a poem called 'April,' although it was March. It was a fancy poem about javelins and leopards and lights through trees like arrows and a line that said: 'The little voices of the rivers change.' I thought it up in and out of the light and the shade of the Forties, between Fifth and Sixth avenues, and typed it on Lax's typewriter in the New Yorker office, and showed it to Mark Van Doren in a subway station."

- *Cistercian Contemplatives.* Trappist, Kentucky: Abbey of Gethsemani, 1948.

    Merton sent the book to Sister Thérèse Lentfoehr with the following inscription: "That she may pray for the writer of this pamphlet & obtain for him the grace to put into practice what he describes." This short guide to the Trappist way of life appeared in January 1948. It is a good example of the kind of writing the Order wanted from him — expository, definite, factual, and devout.

Holograph draft of "For My Brother: Reported Missing in Action, 1943."

- *Figures for an Apocalypse.* New York: New Directions, 1948.

    This volume of poetry was to cause Merton much anguish. James Laughlin sent T. S. Eliot copies, and a year later had to report to Merton that Eliot found the poetry inadequately revised and Merton to be a poet of uneven quality. Merton seriously considered giving up writing poetry. Part of Merton's vision was apocalyptic. This volume contains images of cities laid waste and warnings of false prophets. Hope is to be found in the works of nature and the fullness of a spiritually informed life. Sure in his commitment to the contemplative life, Merton ends the volume with an essay, "Poetry and the Contemplative Life," in which he argues that poetry may actually hamper the spiritual growth of the contemplative author.

    Gift of the Estate of Del Harwood

- Autograph letter signed, to Mark Van Doren, 2 p. Trappist, Kentucky, March 30, 1948.

    In his essay on the problem of reconciling the contemplative life and the life of a poet, Merton came to the conclusion that it might be advisable to give up writing in order to pursue the aim of contemplative life. In this letter, thanking Van Doren for his kind comments about *Figures for an Apocalypse,* he goes on to explain that he is "beginning to see everything in a strangely different light." Shying away from any abstract solution to the problem, Merton adopts an individualistic, empiric approach: "I — and every other person in the world — *must* say: 'I have my own special, peculiar testimony which no one else ever has had or ever will have. There

THE SEVEN STORY MOUNTAIN

I

PRISONER'S BASE

i

On a January night in the mountains of the south of France that are called the Pyrenees, along the Catalan border, in a land grown old with violence and in a year of a great war, I came into the world. It was ~~nineteen-fifteen~~ 1915. I was born into a ~~land~~ world which was the image of hell full of ~~enemies,~~ men like myself, born to love God ~~and~~ but hating Him: idolaters, trying to draw all things into their own emptiness the way God draws them into His fullness. ~~Therefore they were all killing one another and the world was the image of hell.~~ I came out of the womb as I had lain in it, curled about my own center, contemplating not God but myself.

¶ The rainy land to which I came was quiet enough in the ~~territory~~ town of Prades by which I entered it. Yet not so many hundred miles away the muddy ditches were full of men's blood, and the dead horses rotted among the ruined seventy-fives in the grey deforested acres of the Marne and of Champagne.

There were too many people like me in the world, with souls that were images of God, yes, but distorted and without likeness after the manner of those crooked mirrors ~~you see~~ at Coney Island.

¶ ~~One would have thought that~~ I should have been extremely happy in my life, considering the natural gifts with which I was born.

My father was an artist. He painted like Cézanne, and understood the southern French landscape the way Cézanne did -- a way that is

First page of the typewritten draft of "The Seven Storey Mountain," 1948.

exists for me a particular goal, a fulfillment which must be all my own—nobody else's—& it does not really identify that destiny to put it under some category—'poet'—'monk'—'hermit.'"

- "The Seven Storey Mountain." Typewritten manuscript, with autograph corrections, 788 p. [1948].

  This unedited version was given by Merton to Sister Thérèse Lentfoehr. The opening section, "Prisoner's Base," presented the book's editor, Robert Giroux, with the most serious editorial problems. As Giroux writes, "It was 'preachy,' long-winded, and much too abstract. [I] convinced him that readers knowing nothing about him would be put off. I made suggestions, and Merton rewrote it several times." The manuscript also contains twenty-three typescript pages which were deleted from the original 684-page version.

- *The Seven Storey Mountain.* New York: Harcourt, Brace & Company, 1948.

  This novel was published on October 4, 1948, at a time when Merton was a little-known writer who had been living a medieval life in a Trappist monastery in Kentucky. There was certainly no expectation that the book would achieve success, even with the endorsements of Evelyn Waugh, Clifton Fadiman, Graham Greene, Clare Boothe Luce, and Fulton J. Sheen; however, soon after publication the sales began to increase to best-selling proportions. Clearly this story of a worldly young man, on the verge of achieving fame and material reward, who rejects it all in favor of a hard life of prayer and fasting, struck the imagination of the post-war reading public.

  Gift of Robert M. Shepherd

- Portrait photograph of Merton at the time *The Seven Storey Mountain* was published [1949].

- *The Spirit of Simplicity.* Trappist, Kentucky: Abbey of Gethsemani, 1948.

  Inscribed to Sister Thérèse Lentfoehr, "whose poems breath the purest simplicity." In April 1948 the Abbey of Our Lady of Gethsemani published this translation of the report on the "basic legislation about poverty, fasting, enclosure, silence, etc., laid down by...the General Chapter of 1925." The translation and commentary is credited to "A Cistercian Monk." The "Monk" was now the internationally known best-selling author of *The Seven Storey Mountain.* The text is illustrated with twelve sepia photographs of ancient and modern Cistercian architecture and a detailed sketch of a typical abbey in the twelfth century.

- *What is Contemplation?* Holy Cross, Indiana: Saint Mary's College, 1948.

  Inscribed to Sister Thérèse Lentfoehr. The first book to appear with Merton's name on it after *The Seven Storey Mountain* was this small volume on contemplation. The thoughts expressed in this pamphlet were later to be developed into *Seeds of Contemplation.* Merton believed that each Christian must come to realize that contemplation and interior solitude are basic to any union with God and that the "seeds of contemplation and sanctity have been planted" in all men's souls.

- Edward Rice. Two photographs of Merton at the time of his ordination [1949].

    Although a world-famous author and ordained priest, these photographs show Merton's sense of fun as well as his youth.

- "Seeds of Contemplation." Typewritten manuscript, with autograph corrections, 139 p. 1949.

    The first version of *Seeds of Contemplation*. Shown is a page from the chapter "Things in their Identity," in which Merton explains that true individuality is contingent upon our free acceptance of God's will.

- *Seeds of Contemplation*. New York: New Directions, 1949.

    This book and its companion volume, *New Seeds of Contemplation,* are classics of spirituality and mark the pinnacle of Merton's achievements. These reflections on the contemplative life are meant to offer comfort and guidance. Merton's insights into the nature of the spiritual life are more accessible, because they are rendered in a contemporary voice, than those of St. Térèsa of Avila or St. John of the Cross. Claiming no originality, Merton speaks to us of matters such as war, fear, hatred, freedom, and love. The honesty of his voice, his insights, and his deep devotion to the word of God combine with his natural gifts as a writer to produce a work that is both readable and inspiring.

    Gift of Helen Hall Kellogg

- *Gethsemani Magnificat*. Trappist, Kentucky: Abbey of Gethsemani, 1949.

    On the feast of St. Thomas the Apostle, December 21, in 1848, a group of monks from the French monastery of Our Lady of Melleray established a new monastery in the rural hills of Kentucky, calling it the Abbey of Our Lady of Gethsemani. The fourteen-hundred-acre property is locted in a valley southwest of Bardstown. This simple book gives a history of the Cistercian Order and an introduction to the Cistercian way of life in celebration of the one hundredth anniversary of Gethsemani.

- Typewritten letter signed, to Mark Van Doren, 2 p. Trappist, Kentucky, April 8, 1949.

    Inviting Van Doren down to his ordination on May 26, Merton expresses his sense of wonder at the priesthood. "This was what I was always supposed to wear, and everything else, so far, had been something of a disguise." In a postscript Merton promises to send Van Doren "a special boxed edition of *Seeds of Contemplation*." Dom James Fox adds an autograph note confirming the date of Father Louis's ordination and stamps in ink his characteristic closing: "All for Jesus thru Mary with a smile."

- Photograph of Merton being ordained at the Abbey Church of Our Lady of Gethsemani, May 26, 1949.

Merton being ordained at the Abbey Church of Gethsemani, 1949.

The Monk and Teacher: 1950–1958

Throughout the 1950s Merton struggled with his commitment to the communal life of the monastery. He desired increased solitude and seriously considered transferring to a more eremitic order, such as the Camaldolese or the Carthusians. However, he remained at Gethsemani and took on positions of greater responsibility. In 1951 he was appointed master of scholastics and in 1955 master of novices. Both of these positions kept him extremely busy, but he continued to keep his private journals, write poems and essays, and broaden his private study.

- "Waters of Siloe. Prologue." Typewritten manuscript, with autograph corrections, 15 p. [1949].

    "This is the rejected prologue of *Waters of Siloe* — replaced by the one now in the book," Merton informs Sister Thérèse Lentfoehr. Actually the prologue which appears in the book was written first. When Merton sent the manuscript to the publisher he neglected to send the prologue. When the publisher asked for a prologue, Merton, dissatisfied with the one he had originally written, wrote this new prologue and sent both versions to the publisher, who decided to print the original version.

- *The Waters of Siloe*. New York: Harcourt, Brace & Company, 1949.

    Dedicated to Evelyn Waugh, this is one of Merton's most successful assigned writing projects. It is a history of the Cistercian Order from its beginning in the twelfth century, as a reform of Benedictine monasticism, up to the present day. Merton's ability to tell a story, and his obvious love of the Order, make this a highly readable and entertaining book. Shown is a page of photographs with an obvious note of bathos introduced by "Bulldozer, Gethsemani." The increased use of mechanized farm equipment at Gethsemani irritated Merton.

- Evelyn Waugh. Autograph letter signed, to Thomas Merton, 2 p. Pier's Court, Gloucestershire, August 30, 1950.

    Waugh edited *The Seven Storey Mountain* for British publication under the title *Elected Silence* (a phrase from Gerard Manley Hopkins). In this letter he thanks Merton for taking "my editing of *Waters of Siloe* in such good part. (I was paid in church candles for the dining-room table.)" After informing Merton of the birth of another son, Septimus, and a proposed trip to the United States ("Too brief...to hope to get to Kentucky"), he adds that the unusual writing paper comes from Naples.

- *The Tears of the Blind Lions.* New York: New Directions, 1949.

    The difficulty of writing poetry about the contemplative life is answered by this volume of poems. Here we find a calmer Merton, no longer trying to put the world at a distance. Although a slim volume, containing only seventeen poems, Merton thought it superior to the earlier *Figures for an Apocalypse.* Clearly Merton was improving his poetic skills, and for two of the poems in this volume, "St. Malachy" and "From the Legend of St. Clement," Merton was one of two writers to receive the Harriet Monroe Memorial Prize for 1949. Leon Bloy's observation, "When those who love God try to talk about Him, their words are blind lions looking for springs in the desert," is the source for the title of this collection of poems.

    Gift of Eugene P. Sheehy

- Watercolor head of Christ [ca. 1949–1953].

- Pen and pencil drawing of a cross [ca. 1949–1953].

- *What are these Wounds?* Milwaukee: The Bruce Publishing Company, 1950.

    This biography of St. Lutgarde (1182–1246) is based on *Vita Lutgardis* by Thomas of Cantimpré, a contemporary of St. Thomas Aquinas. Merton did not think highly of this work, rating it as one of his worst books. The unfortunate design of the dust jacket was, perhaps, an omen.

- *The Ascent to Truth.* New York: Harcourt, Brace and Company, 1951.

    This study of the mysticism of St. John of the Cross is Merton's only systematic theological work. Lacking any autobiographical element or scope for creative language, the book becomes a somewhat strained attempt to analyze and explain that which is inexplicable, "the hidden or secret knowledge of God that is granted to the soul which is united to him by love," as Merton defines mysticism. Shortly after this book was finished Merton was appointed master of scholastics at Gethsemani.

    Gift of Robert M. Shepherd

- "Saint John of the Ladder." Typewritten manuscript, with autograph corrections and additions, 9 p. [ca. 1951].

    Saint John Climacus (ca. 570–649), ascetic writer and Abbot of Sinai, is best remembered for his celebrated spiritual work *Ladder of Paradise.* Merton enjoys the blustering, no-nonsense style of St. John Climacus, calling him a "kind of sixth century Hemingway" who writes of the many ways of unmasking the Devil and "busting him in the teeth." However, the line which Merton considers "more influential than all the rest of the book put together" is "let the remembrance of Jesus be present with each breath, and then you will know the value of solitude."

- "Texts from Saint Bernard." Typewritten manuscript, 1 p. [1952].

    At the request of Sister Thérèse Lentfoehr, Merton selected these quotations from the writings of St. Bernard to be used on a series of bookmarks, which were never printed. The quotes are suitably profound, sometimes even slyly humorous:

Pen and pencil drawing of a cross by Merton, ca. 1949–1953.

"If you wish to know Jesus you will find Him sooner by following Him than by reading books."

■ Autograph manuscript notebook, 112 p. 1948–1949.

Originally titled "The Whale and the Ivy," this notebook contains part of *The Sign of Jonas*. Throughout, Merton checks entries to be included in the book while others are crossed out in blue pencil. Sister Thérèse Lentfoehr acted as Merton's secretary for this book and typed out the manuscript. Shown is the entry for November 30, 1948, describing the visit by Evelyn Waugh to the Abbey of Gethsemani.

■ *The Sign of Jonas.* New York: Harcourt, Brace & Company, 1953.

To live as both a writer and a monk was difficult for Merton. He finally decided to accept the paradox as part of his humanity. However, during his early years at Gethsemani he was troubled by his dual vocation. This book is composed of entries from his journals from December 1946 to July 1952. In it Merton traces his spiritual and artistic growth. The strong, steady, ascetic voice of the young monk in *The Seven Story Mountain* is seen evolving into a voice capable of exploring the many aspects of monastic spiritual life and the life of a modern writer.

■ Pen and ink drawing of a monk [ca. 1952].

This drawing closely resembles the one which appeared in the *Saturday Review* in 1952, which was a reprint of a sketch drawn to accompany a review of *The Sign of Jonas* by William Habich for the *Louisville Courier-Journal*. The face of the angel appears also in his autograph notebook for 1939–1944.

■ *Bread in the Wilderness.* New York: New Directions, 1953.

As poetry and song, the Psalms held a special meaning for Merton. In this book he meditates on their meaning and use as tools which the soul can use to attain communion with God. Pictures of the famous crucifix, *Devot Christ* at Perpignan, France, accompany the text. The inscription to Sister Thérèse Lentfoehr reads: "...because she has been a valuable companion and helper in the wilderness through which we voyage to the Promised Land. May the Divine Savior guide us onward in the desert!"

■ "Saints Peter and Paul." Typewritten manuscript notes, with autograph corrections and additions, 5 p. [1953].

As Merton says in these notes for a sermon, "Martyrs are not made by the wickedness of men, but by divine necessity." Merton makes the point that each Christian must "die" for Christ, in the sense that each person must reject the evil of this world and his own self-importance. He tells his fellow monks to learn to love their own nothingness, to live as do the sparrows and embrace the implications of Matthew 10:29: "Are not two sparrows sold for a penny?"

■ Typewritten letter signed, to Mark Van Doren, 2 p. Trappist, Kentucky, August 11, 1953.

and I think [...] ordered
to exterior action in so far as that action can ultimately contribute to
contemplation — at least [...]. Or to put it in another way, [...]
order external action in such a way that it interferes as little as possible with
the contemplative life. St John's [...] on direction, or when to give up
meditation, [...] "3 [...] blind guides" (Living Flame) shows you the Gift of
Counsel at work. Counsel says — "Venite seorsum et aquiescite pusillum."

Nov. 30. F. of St Andrew. Tues.

It is already Advent. [...] the last minister before the retreat the novices are
practising some sweet polyphony for the small centenary celebration we are
supposed to be holding on December 21st. Bishop Cotton is alleged to be going to say the
Pontifical Mass & Archbishop Floersh to sing the high Mass but nothing has been
said about anyone being ordained subdeacon by either of them.

I am terrified that Archbishop Floersh may want to talk to me — & will then
discover that I know no theology.

* * *

Evelyn Waugh arrived Saturday night after everyone was in bed and left
Sunday at noon in a storm of rain. I expected him to be taller and more
dashing; but he was very nice and very friendly.

The first thing he did was to reproach me with the fact that the house was
so hot. He said it made the book all wrong. The lay brothers have got that
huge boiler working now, & that is the cause of all the trouble. We are still in
summer clothing & yet I sweat in choir.

E. Waugh said Hollywood was very dull. He expected great jewels and
thought everything would surely be done with parades of elephants but found that the
people were just business men doing their business & that there was no
entertainment anywhere except in the cemetery which, he said, he visited
every day.

He offered to send us books but said that "the Heart of the Matter" &
"the Loved One" were not proper material for our refectory.

The lady in True Life & Fortune who arranged his itinerary for him
routed him from Cincinnatti to Louisville via Washington D.C.

Page from Merton's notebook containing drafts of "The Sign of Jonas," 1948–1949.

- Photograph of Merton *(first row, center)* as master of novices [1955].

- "Dans le Desert de Dieu." Offprint from *Temoignages*. Pierre-Qui-Vire, France: Benedictines [1955].

    Merton's desire for solitude and his writings on the subject were not, at first, readily accepted by his Order. On the first page of this offprint, which he sent to Sister Thérèse Lentfoehr, he writes: "This is rare, controversial, has not appeared in English, only in French & Italian — & is very personal."

- Typewritten letter signed, to Mark Van Doren, 2 p. Trappist, Kentucky, December 30, 1955.

    After informing Van Doren that he has been made master of novices, giving him "practically a small kingdom of my own," Merton confides to his friend the recurrence of his old desire for solitude: "Again the old wrestling, more awful than before, about solitude. . . . I even got as far as Rome (I mean with pestering letters) and finally the highest Superiors under the Pope calmed me down and told me to stay here." Merton also mentions the fire tower which the abbot was allowing him to use as a type of hermitage.

- "Life at Gethsemani." Autograph outline, 4 p.; design for pamphlet, 23 p. [1955].

    Throughout his monastic life Merton was assigned various writing tasks, many of which he found less than stimulating, but which he completed with professional grace. This pamphlet serves as a general introduction to the Trappist way of life, as well as a subtle enticement for those young men thinking of a religious life. "Do you seek all this?" the writer asks. "Then one thing more is necessary: *Courage*." The outline of the monk's day shows, in part, the difficulty of the life.

- "Sentences." Typewritten manuscript, with autograph corrections, 31 p. [1952].

    This series of 121 random reflections are meant to be glimpses of truth, moments of illumination which, as Merton says in his preface, are like the fragile light of a match. Sensing that this form had greater possibilities, he expanded it till he had enough to make the book *No Man Is an Island*.

    Part of Merton's duties at the monastery was to help with fire fighting and fire patrol. When the cow barn burnt down it was consumed with such terrible beauty that Merton sought to capture both the physical reality of the fire and also the spiritual meaning of the event. He includes a typed copy of the poem "Elegy for the Monastery Barn" with his letter; the poem was published in *The Strange Islands*.

- *The Last of the Fathers*. New York: Harcourt, Brace & Company, 1954.

    On the occasion of the eighth centenary of the death of St. Bernard of Clairvaux (1090–1153), Pope Pius XII issued an encyclical letter. This book was commissioned by the Order, since St. Bernard was the great restorer and promoter of the Cistercians in twelfth-century Europe. Michael Mott, Merton's official biographer, detects

"certain telling failures of nerve" on Merton's part in dealing with this active proponent of the Crusades.
Gift of Morris H. Saffron

■ "Notes on Sacred Art." Typewritten manuscript, with autograph corrections, 28 p. 1954.

As part of a series of conferences given to the scholastics at Gethsemani on the nature of sacred art (later shortened and published in *Jubilee*), Merton discussed the nature of Cistercian monastic design. After giving an example of the design of a twelfth-century monastery, Merton offers his own plan for a modern monastery, taking full note of the need to place at a distance all the modern machines which so disturb the peace of the monastic setting. "NO VEHICLE OR MACHINE GETS FURTHER THAN THIS," makes Merton's intention clear.

Merton (first row, center) as master of novices, 1955.

- "Viewpoints." Typewritten manuscript, with autograph corrections and additions, 194 p. [ca. 1954].

    In this work, published as *No Man Is an Island,* Merton meditates on various Christian themes fundamental to the interior life: "conscience; vocation; sacrifice; charity & mercy; sincerity; prayer and recollection; silence and solitude." Throughout, Merton stresses the dual aspects of Christian life: the need to find oneself in order to find others; to surrender the will in order to accept the will of God; to love God through a true love of self; to abandon in order to gain.

- *No Man Is an Island.* New York: Harcourt, Brace & Company, 1955.

    This sequel to *Seeds of Contemplation* is meant to be "simpler, more fundamental, and more detailed." Growing out of Merton's teaching as master of novices, it is dedicated to scholastics studying for the priesthood.

    Gift of Robert M. Shepherd

- "Abelard." Autograph manuscript, 13 p. [ca. 1957].

    Peter Abelard (1079-1142) is perhaps best known today as a romantic figure due to his love affair with Heloise, the niece of Fulbert, Canon of Notre-Dame, and subsequent retirement to the monastery of St.-Denis. He was, however, one of the greatest Catholic philosophers and theologians. A controversial figure, his independence and analytic ability aroused the hostility of the authoritarian St. Bernard, who denounced his teaching to the bishops of France. Merton admired Abelard, and in his conferences and talks said that he always preferred men of passion.

- *The Silent Life.* New York: Farrar, Straus & Cudahy, 1957.

    Merton was very much concerned with an analysis of monasticism and the role played by solitude in fulfilling the monk's ultimate goal of a perfect union with God. After considering certain aspects of the monastic life, Merton discusses some of the major monastic orders. He draws a distinction between the cenobitic tradition of the Cistercians and the Benedictines and the eremitic tradition of the Carthusians and the Camaldolese. Merton stresses the role of silence and solitude in his inscription to Sister Thérèse Lentfoehr: "May the word who spoke in silence at Bethlehem always speak silently in the peace of our hearts."

- *The Strange Islands.* New York: New Directions, 1957.

    Greeted with mediocre reviews, this volume of poetry is transitional. It contains formal lyrics, confessional poems, and a verse drama, "The Tower of Babel."

- "The Tower of Babel." Typewritten manuscript (carbon), with autograph additions, 4 p.; autograph manuscript, 13 p. 1954.

    Published as the second section of *The Strange Islands,* this verse play deals with the abuse of language in modern society and the corruption of the world through love of self. Significantly, Merton does not choose to reject the world, as he had in so much of his early poetry, but adopts a tone of compassion and hope. Starting from "A Responsory. (for Paul Hindemith)," Merton expanded the poem greatly. The drama was performed on the radio broadcast "The Catholic Hour," January 27, 1957.

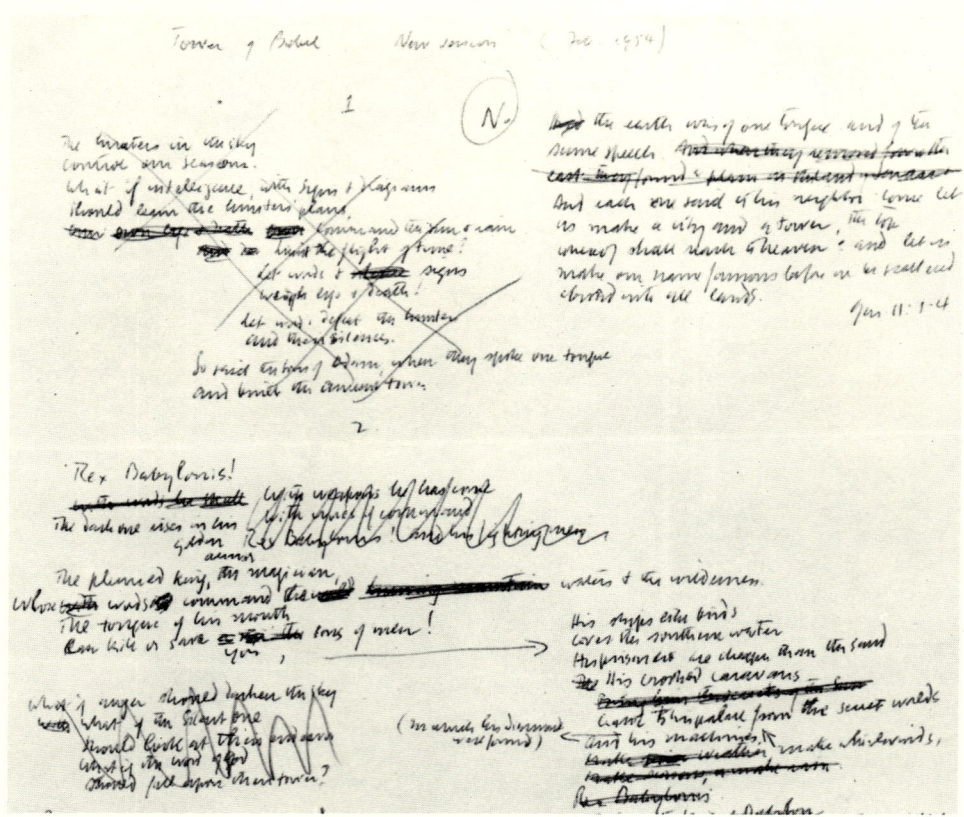

Page from holograph draft of "The Tower of Babel," 1954.

■ *The Tower of Babel.* Woodcuts by Gerhard Marcks. Hamburg: James Laughlin, 1957. Number 158 of 250 copies. Signed by Merton and Marcks.
Frederic Bancroft Fund

■ ["Prayer"]. Typewritten manuscript, 2 p. 1956.
In this prayer Merton reminds himself of his faults and his duties. His sense of guilt is heightened by an uncertainty about the future: "Perhaps the time is shorter than I think.... Make my remaining days rich in good works and in loving faith and take me to You in mercy the moment I die...."

■ Photograph of Merton and Mark Van Doren at the Abbey of Gethsemani [ca. 1957].

■ "Thoughts in Solitude." Typewritten manuscript signed (carbon), 67 p. [ca. 1958].
Influenced by Max Picard's *World of Silence,* Merton wrote these notes on various aspects of the solitary life and the role of silence. Initially arranged as a series of thirty-seven meditations, Merton soon realized that such organization belied the true nature

of the work. Therefore, these spontaneous, heavily existential thoughts are presented without organization. Merton referred to this version as the "original original, the first draft notes, which at the last moment I tried to get them to publish last fall. I thought at the time it was a better version, but probably it wouldn't seem so to the general reader." Published by Farrar, Straus & Cudahy on April 8, 1958.

■ *Prometheus: A Meditation.* Lexington: Privately printed at the Margaret I. King Library Press, University of Kentucky, 1958. One of 150 copies printed under the supervision of Victor and Caroline Hammer.

Prometheus is a metaphor for the state of modern man's soul. We are so fixed on trying to find our true identity in the falsities of the world that we gladly reject the unquestioning love and understanding of God. We die in despair rather than live in grace. For Merton, the path to enlightenment is expressed in his inscription to Sister Thérèse Lentfoehr: "On our Lady's Assumption since Mary knew that the way to ascend is to descend."

■ *Nativity Kerygma.* Trappist, Kentucky: Abbey of Gethsemani, 1958.

This proclamation, or *kerygma,* of the birth of Christ and His immanence was designed by Stanley Morison, with artwork and layout by Frank Kacmarcik. In the "Author's Note" Merton expressly forbids the selling of copies of this solemn and joyful message, and adds, ". . .they are not offered for sale, they can only be given as a present."

■ "Notes on the Benedictine Rule." Autograph manuscript, 2 p. 1958.

As Merton saw it, at the very heart of the Benedictine idea was the vow of stability, but trying to determine the "meaning and force of Stability [was, in Merton's judgment] perhaps the most difficult point in a study of Benedictine life." Concerned as to how his desire for an eremitic life might conflict with his vow of stability, Merton argues that "there is no solid evidence to show that a hermit attached to the monastery of his profession would violate his vow of stability by leaving the cenobitic life!"

■ "Poetry and Contemplation: a Reappraisal." Typewritten manuscript, with autograph corrections and additions, 26 p. 1958.

This important essay is a revision of an earlier statement of the problem of reconciling two separate vocations — contemplative monk and professional writer. Merton tries to dismiss the conflict by stating that "the earlier problem was, largely, an illusion, created by this division of life into formally separate compartments, of 'action' and 'contemplation.'" His view of the matter is wholly pragmatic. Merton sees no conflict between the spiritual and artistic life. The mystic may, indeed, also be a writer, even though such a person "may be unable to pass on to the superior and most spiritual kind of contemplation, in which the soul rests in God without images, without concepts, without an intermediary."

■ "'The News I Read as a Secular.'" Typewritten manuscript, with autograph corrections and additions, 3 vol. 1939–1941.

These binders contain the manuscript from which *The Secular Journal* was edited. As can be seen, the original journal is far larger than the printed version.

- *The Secular Journal of Thomas Merton.* New York: Farrar, Strauss & Cudahy, 1959.

    Although published after Merton had been in the Order for seventeen years, this journal was written while Merton was in his mid-twenties, teaching at St. Bonaventure College. The journal deals with themes of universal human guilt in war and the illusion of material success, and details the struggle of Merton over his choice of whether to enter the monastery and the implications of such a choice on his life as a writer.

- "Art and Worship." Typewritten manuscript, with autograph corrections and additions, 40 p. [1959].

    From his lectures and seminars on aesthetics as master of novices, Merton planned to write a book on contemporary religious art. However, the project was abandoned and parts later published as essays. The proliferation of bad religious art bothered Merton. He saw no reason why the contemporary artist could not achieve the greatest art while treating a religious subject with proper dignity and sanctity. In this he was encouraged by the chapter on sacred art in the *Constitution on the Liturgy* of the Second Vatican Council.

- "What Shall I Do?" Typewritten manuscript, with autograph corrections, 26 p. [1958].

    The first version of the translation and introduction to the writings of the Desert Fathers, selected from the *Verba Seniorum* in Migne's *Latin Patrology,* volume 73.

- *What Ought I to Do?* Lexington: Stamperia del Santuccio, 1959. One of fifty numbered copies.

    Merton had a special love of the early Christian cenobites and hermits. In their lives and writings Merton found a deep source of spiritual inspiration, as well as a strong link between East and West. Their proverbs and tales, often Zen-like in their paradoxical phrasing on how to live the Christian life, fascinated Merton. In 1961 New Directions published these translations under the title *Wisdom of the Desert Fathers.*

The Public Years: 1959–1964

*I*n the 1960s Merton reached out to the world in many ways, while continuing his efforts to be allowed to retire to a hermitage. Merton embraced the study of Eastern religious traditions, especially Zen Buddhism; he took an active lead in the anti-nuclear movement; he spoke out for racial justice and an end to the arms race; he interpreted the message of Vatican II; he wrote on the need for monastic renewal; his poetry became increasingly experimental and he encouraged other poets by publishing a little magazine; above all, he spoke with love and concern about the nature of the human soul and its need for solitude, peace, nature, and the acceptance of God's grace.

- Aldous Huxley. Typewritten letter signed, to Thomas Merton, 2 p. Los Angeles, January 10, 1959.

  Intrigued by Huxley's article on the effects of LSD and mescaline, Merton wrote asking him to clarify some points dealing with the mystical state produced by these drugs. Specifically, Merton was troubled by the lack of freedom and spontaneity in any drug-inspired mystical state. Huxley's reply addresses Merton's questions but without denying the validity of the mystical experience based on drug use.

- Luis A. Somoza. Typewritten letter signed, to Thomas Merton, 3 p. Managua, Nicaragua, July 18, 1959.

  On July 4, 1959, Merton wrote to Luis Somoza, president of Nicaragua, to appeal to him not to take bloody reprisals against those who had taken part in a failed revolt. Such an action "can only blacken your good name and bring further sorrow and violence upon Nicaragua," he tells Somoza. In his reply, Somoza claims that Merton is acting upon misleading press reports and that "the authorities have proceeded with all humanity, they fed them, rendered them medical attention and lodged them in the jails."

- "The Pasternak Affair." Typewritten manuscript, with autograph corrections, 3 p. [1959].

  In 1958 Merton wrote to Boris Pasternak and sent him a copy of *Prometheus: A Meditation* under separate cover. Merton corresponded with and supported Pasternak until the latter's death in 1960. These manuscript inserts are for his essay on Pasternak which was published in *Disputed Questions*. Not wishing to further aggravate the tensions surrounding Pasternak's acceptance, then rejection, of the Nobel Prize for Literature, Merton focuses on the universal aspects of Pasternak's struggle with the Soviet authorities. With total commitment to the redeeming power of love

> LIKE EVERYTHING ELSE IN THE CHRISTIAN LIFE,
> the vocation to solitude can be understood only
> within the perspective of God's mercy to man
> in the Incarnation of Christ. If there is any
> such thing as a Christian hermit, then he must
> be a man who has a special function in the
> mystical body of Christ — a hidden and spiritu-
> al function, and perhaps all the more vital
> because more hidden. But this social function of
> the hermit, precisely because it has to be in-
> visible, cannot be allowed in any way to detract
> from his genuinely solitary character. On the
> contrary, his function in the Christian commu-
> nity is the paradoxical one of living outwardly
> separated from the community. And this,
> whether he is conscious of it or not, is a witness
> to the completely transcendental character
> of the Christian mystery of our unity in Christ.
> The hermit remains to put us on our guard
> against our natural obsession with the visible,
> social and communal forms of Christian life
> which tend at times to be inordinately active,
> and become deeply involved in the life of
> secular non-Christian society. The average
> Christian is in the world but not of it. But in case
> he might be likely to forget this — or worse still
> in case he might never come to know it at all —
> there must be men who have completely re-
> nounced the world: men who are neither in the
> world nor of it. In our day, when «the world» is
> everywhere, even and perhaps especially in
> the desert, the hermit retains his unique and
> mysterious function. But he will fulfill it per-
>
> 1   haps

Page from the Stamperia del Santuccio edition of The Solitary Life, *1960.*

and a deep understanding of human nature, Pasternak is seen as a man of spiritual insight, able to transcend the political debate and speak to all men. In 1973 the King Library Press at the University of Kentucky published *Pasternak-Merton: Six Letters, 1958-1960.*

■ "Mount Athos: a famous Trappist discusses a spiritual center of Orthodox Christianity." Printed article, *Jubilee,* August 1959, with autograph corrections, 5 p.; typewritten inserts, with autograph corrections, 10 p.

– 40 –

For Merton, Mount Athos represented the ideal monastic setting: "What if someday there were to be an Athos for the Western Church, the Western world? Some island, some mountain jutting out into the sea, a 'nation' of contemplatives with room enough for Benedictines and Carthusians and Cistercians and Camaldolese, for cenobites and hermits...." In this article Merton allows his frustration with modern monastic life to show: "What we really ought to do is what the first monks did: go off somewhere into the wilderness (approved by a qualifed director) and see how long and how well we can stand it — with or without companions."

■ *The Solitary Life.* Lexington: Stamperia del Santuccio, 1960. One of sixty numbered copies printed by Victor Hammer.

Merton believed that the hermit did have a place within a Cistercian monastery. The Cistercian hermit serves to remind the community of the "completely transcendental character of the Christian mystery of our unity in Christ." Always attracted by the paradoxical, Merton embraced the various contrary elements in the idea of becoming a hermit within a cenobitic community, and was able to reconcile himself to the contradictions involved in being a contemplative monk and a highly productive and successful author.

■ *Disputed Questions.* New York: Farrar, Straus & Cudahy, 1960.

Merton's desire to communicate the nature of the spiritual truths he discovered in his contemplative life drove him to engage the world. The dual process of withdrawal and engagement resulted in works of profound truth and insight. Nowhere is Merton's engagement with the world more evident than in this challenging book. Merton asks questions about identity, truth, and value, and answers with the clear voice of a man who has a deep concern for the integrity of language and a love of mankind. A primary issue for Merton is the proper relation of the individual to society. He warns us against the false individuality that isolates and alienates, and asks us to find ourselves by exploring our inner lives: "In order to find our own souls we have to enter into our own solitude and learn to live with ourselves."

Gift of Robert M. Shepherd

■ "Let the Poor Man Speak." Typewritten manuscript, with autograph corrections and additions, 10 p. [1960].

In 1959 Don Primo Mazzolari wrote a book on poverty, *La Parola ai Poveri,* which greatly impressed Merton. This translation of a few pages from the book together with Merton's blunt thoughts on the subject of poverty and social inequality was published in *Jubilee,* October 1960: "I translated these few pages from this remarkable book because I am ashamed of myself and the world in which I live."

■ "Liturgy and Spiritual Personalism." Typewritten manuscript, with autograph corrections and additions, 18 p. [1960].

Merton saw the opposition between public and private prayer as fundamentally misleading. Using the Greek concept of *parrhesia,* or the right to free speech before the assembly, Merton argues that the liturgy is the manifestation of all that is best in private prayer. It is the freely given expression of communal love, an act of free individuals proclaiming their communality of belief and their gift of love. Merton wishes to dispel notions that the liturgy is a group act in which the individual is submerged. He broadens his theme to indict the lip service given to freedom and individuality in contemporary America: "We who have made such a cult of originality, experiment, personal commitment and individual creativity now find ourselves among the least individual, the least original and the least personal of all the people on the face of the earth."

- Typewritten letter signed, to Sister Thérèse Lentfoehr, 2 p. Trappist, Kentucky, September 12, 1960.

  "Notes for a Philosophy of Solitude" in *Disputed Questions* was Merton's clearest statement on this troublesome issue. The censors did not like what he had to say; in fact, Merton tells Sister Thérèse not to mention that part of the essay which had been printed by Victor Hammer at the Stamperia del Santuccio Press in Lexington, Kentucky: "It does not even exist officially. It must not begin to do so." Clearly, Merton was still intent on pursuing an eremitical life within the Cistercian Order.

- "The Ox Mountain Parable of Meng Tzu." Typewritten manuscript, with autograph corrections and additions, 3 p. 1961.

  This story of the Ox Mountain, stripped bare of its forest, is used by Meng Tzu (Mencius) and Merton to emphasize the destruction of man's natural goodness by ego and passions. We are like a lush forest but through our misguided actions we destroy what God and nature have sown. Merton liked any examples from Eastern thought which emphasized a communal approach between East and West, Catholic and non-Catholic.

- *The Ox Mountain Parable of Meng Tzu.* Lexington: Stamperia del Santuccio, 1960. Limited edition. Published by Victor Hammer.

  Inscribed to Sister Thérèse Lentfoehr: "This deep and comforting parable of man's vocation, which is not without an obscure reference to Advent & to the coming of the One who restored the wooded mountain as a new Eden."

- *The Behavior of Titans.* New York: New Directions, 1961.

  Merton contends that the threat to the world posed by men of self-will, lovers of power, is aided by our inaction, our bystanding. In this book Merton warns us, through the use of myth, philosophy, fiction, and poetry, of the possible disintegration of our world and the decay of our sensibilities.

- Photographs of the Zen garden at the Abbey of Gethsemani [ca. 1962].

  In the early 1960s Merton sent Sister Thérèse Lentfoehr these photographs of the Zen garden which he had started shortly after being appointed master of novices in 1955.

- "Christian Ethics and Nuclear War." Typewritten manuscript, with autograph corrections and additions, 12 p. 1961.

  The concept of a "just war" or "justified self-defense" are simply not applicable when it comes to nuclear weapons. Merton's strong views on the subject of nuclear

Merton in a study hut at Gethsemani, early 1960s.

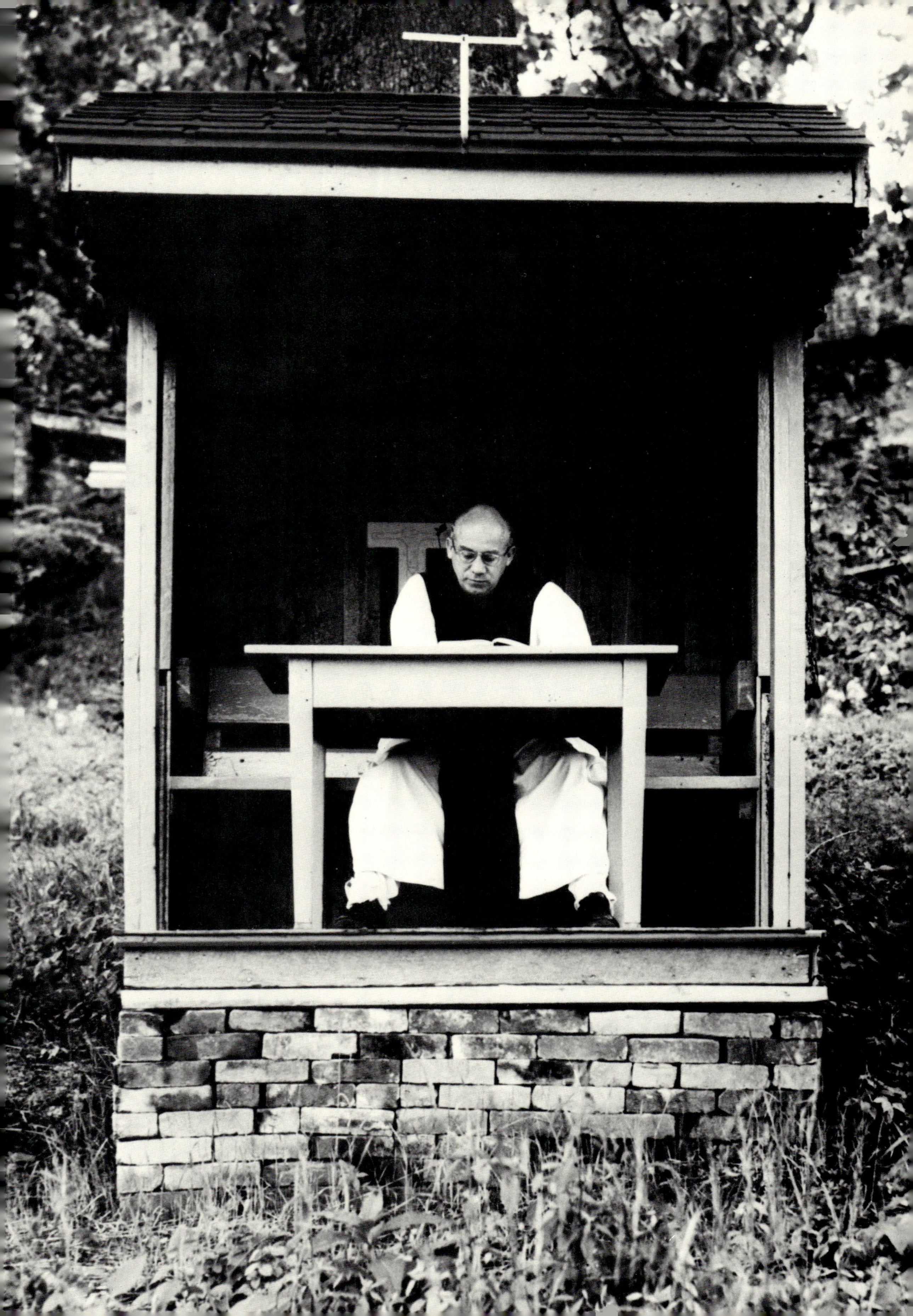

war brought him into conflict with the censors of the Order. In this essay, published in the March 1962 issue of *Catholic Worker* and collected in *Thomas Merton on Peace* (1971), Merton argues that one cannot be both a believing Christian and a believer in nuclear weapons. The moral implications involved in nuclear war are such that the Christian is morally obligated to reject them and their use unequivocally.

- "New Seeds of Contemplation." Typewritten manuscript, with autograph corrections and additions, 78 p. [1961].

- *New Seeds of Contemplation.* New York: New Directions, 1961.

    Perhaps Merton's finest piece of writing, this classic work on the spiritual life is a reconsideration of various themes dealt with in *Seeds of Contemplation.* The evidence of Merton's growth both as a writer and as a man is revealed in the broader treatment and changed tone. No longer is Merton the isolated monk speaking to a world he has rejected. The need for solitude in a world dominated by inhuman forces is central to Merton's argument for change. In the concluding chapter, "The General Dance," Merton places man in relation to the universe and finds that "no despair of ours can alter the reality of things, or strain the joy of the cosmic dance which is always there."

- *Original Child Bomb.* New York: New Directions, 1961. One of five hundred signed copies.

    This chilling prose poem, illustrated by Emil Antonucci, achieves its effects by stripping the language relating to the dropping of the nuclear bomb on Hiroshima to statements of fact and thereby indicting a world.

- Emil Antonucci. Four watercolor illustrations for *Original Child Bomb,* 1961.

    These stark illustrations suitably match the bleak content of the book.

- Typewritten letter signed, to Mark Van Doren, 1 p. Trappist, Kentucky, February 16, 1961.

    Calling his *Original Child Bomb* "a deadpan thing, a simple chaining together of clichés that are frightening," Merton tells Van Doren that he just wants "to say a loud 'No' to missiles and Polaris submarines and everything which sneaks up on a city to destroy it." Merton draws a distinction between justice and mercy: ". . . the just are unjust and those who are justified are so only by mercy received and given."

- Typewritten letter signed, to Mark Van Doren, 1 p. Trappist, Kentucky, May 13, 1961.

    At the Columbia Commencement in June 1961, Mark Van Doren accepted the University Medal for Excellence on behalf of his former student and friend, Thomas Merton (the Reverend M. Louis, O.C.S.O.). With his typical sense of humor, Merton tells Van Doren that he will "sit here [at Gethsemani] with [his] shoes off among the ants and rave at the world" as his former professor accepts the University medal.

- Photograph of Merton in a study hut at Gethsemani [early 1960s].

Title page from Merton's anti-war prose poem, 1961.

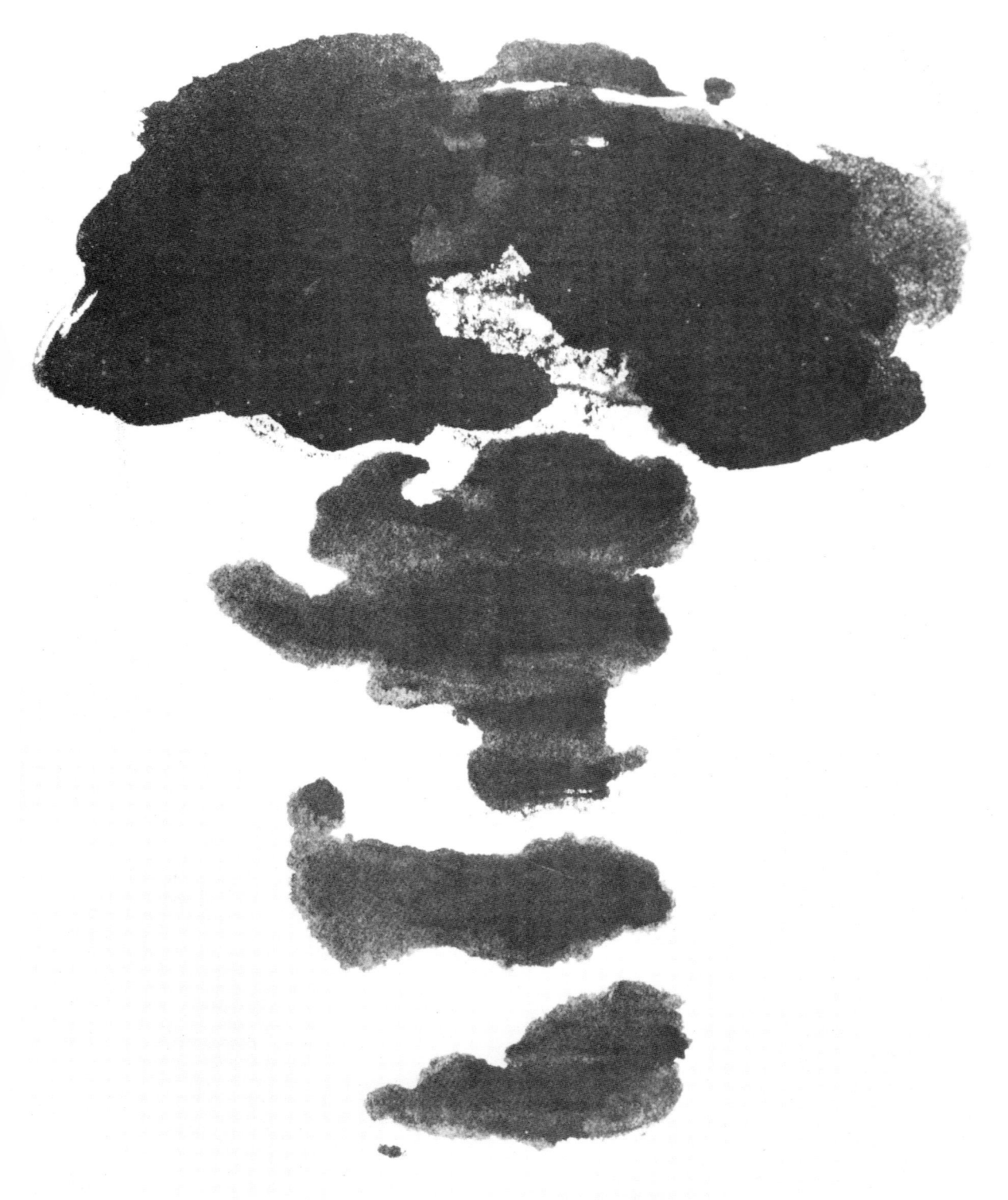

ORIGINAL CHILD BOMB
points for meditation to be scratched on the walls of a cave
THOMAS MERTON

- *A Thomas Merton Reader.* New York: Harcourt, Brace & World, 1962.

    In the introduction to this selection from his writings, Merton confronts the nature of his life as both monk and writer: "I have had to accept that my life is almost totally paradoxical. I have had to learn gradually to get along without apologizing for the fact, even to myself. And perhaps this preface is an indication that I have not yet completely learned. No matter. It is in the paradox itself, the paradox which was and still is a source of insecurity, that I have come to find the greatest security. I have become convinced that the very contradictions in my life are in some ways signs of God's mercy to me."

- "Hagia Sophia": "Dawn. The Hour of Lauds," autograph manuscript, 1 p. [1961]; "High Morning. The Hour of Tierce," typewritten manuscript, with autograph corrections, 1 p. [1961]; autograph introduction to the mimeographed edition of the poem, 1 p. [1962].

    Parts one and three of the four-part poem to the Blessed Virgin Mary. The introduction to the mimeographed edition of the poem explains its genesis and meaning: "In an hour when madness seems to triumph over everything, let us remember that wisdom is always victorious."

- *Hagia Sophia.* Lexington: Stamperia del Santuccio Press, 1978. One of fifty copies.

    This reprint of Victor Hammer's 1962 edition has a printing of the artist's unfinished engraving added. The feminine aspect of God — "the dark, yielding, tender counterpart of the power, justice, creative dynamism of the Father" — is addressed in this prose poem, which grew out of a letter to Victor Hammer. After seeing a triptych painted by Hammer, Merton started to meditate on the meaning of Mary, the mother of God, and her role in the Incarnation. The aspect of mercy and love in all creation is the central theme of this poem, structured around the rhythms of the canonical hours.

- "Clement of Alexandria." Autograph manuscript notes, 6 p. [1962].

    Merton's preliminary notes on Clement's teaching and his thoughts on the function of education.

- *Clement of Alexandria.* New York: New Directions, 1962.

    Clement of Alexandria was a Greek born in the middle of the second century and raised as a pagan. Converted to Christianity by Pantaenus of Alexandria, he founded a school of Christian studies in the city and sought to bring people to Christ by awakening in them the "spark of goodness deposited in them by the Creator." Merton was attracted to Clement as a fellow poet and mystic, and was delighted when he discovered that both Fénelon and Newman had been inspired by Clement's writings.

    Gift of Robert M. Shepherd

- "The Good Samaritan." Typewritten manuscript, with autograph corrections and additions, 11 p. [1962].

Stonnig
Double space.

HAGIA SOPHIA

This poem developed out of a letter written to Victor Hammer in answer to a question about one of his paintings. The painting represented the Blessed Virgin Mary placing a crown upon the head of the child Christ. Victor Hammer said he had no clear way to explain why the Holy Mother should be placing a crown upon her Son. I said that it was most fitting that she should do so, since this represented the Wisdom of God, Hagia Sophia, in the Blessed Virgin, crowning the Divine Son with his human nature. After that Victor Hammer asked me to repeat this explanation in a letter, which I did. When he thought of painting the Text of the letter, I revised it, so that it became a prose poem in honor of Sophia. By this time other personal thoughts about Sophia had found their way into the "elucidation," written at Pinckcourt, 1961. Now the poem has been printed in a limited edition of some fifty copies by Victor Hammer on his press at the Stamperia del Santuccio in Lexington.

[In an hour when madness seems to triumph over everything, let us remember that Wisdom is always victorious. The crown she has placed on the Logos is the crown of eternal Kingship. "For his power is an everlasting power & his kingdom is to all generations" (Daniel 4:31.)

T.M.
January 1962

→ This text has been mimeographed for the sake of those who might not have access to one of the printed copies.

Holograph draft of the introduction to the mimeographed edition of "Hagia Sophia," 1962.

The answers to the questions "Who is my neighbor?" and "Who must I love?" were to be found, for Merton, in an understanding of the concept of *chesed* — mercy, disinterested love, strength, acceptance, and forgiveness. This concept challenges man to act like a saint and is the source of all true love. The parable of the good Samaritan becomes a model in its totality of the concept of *chesed*. This essay was one of Merton's favorites.

- "Red or Dead." Typewritten manuscript, with autograph corrections and additions, 7 p. [1962].

Aggravated by the sophistries of the Cold War, Merton wrote this piece to call our attention to the threat to life and civilization which such slogans hide. Merton argues against the "mentality of defeat" and moral debasement of such a slogan, appealing to us to live up to the ideals of our country and accept the responsibility of thinking rationally. In a postscript, Merton reminds all Christians that the "Atheists have no monopoly on cruelty and violence."

- "Letter of Fulbert of Chartres to King Robert." Autograph manuscript, 2 p. [1963].

The medieval mixture of natural and supernatural evident in this eleventh-century letter fascinated Merton. This translation was published in *Emblems of a Season of Fury* with the suitably grotesque title "What to Do if It Rains Blood."

- *Emblems of a Season of Fury.* New York: New Directions, 1963.

These poems spring directly from Merton's deep social concern. The subjects dealt with include Auschwitz, Birmingham, the bomb, and the refugee. As always, Merton is not simply critical of modern society, but is careful to show us the way to true humanity. The tone, therefore, ranges from the savage irony of "Chant to Be Used in Processions Around a Site with Furnaces" to the simplicity of "Grace's House."

- "Reflections on the Character and Genius of Fénelon." Typewritten manuscript, with autograph corrections, 16 p. [1963].

In this introduction to a selection of François Fénelon's (1651–1715) writings, Merton stresses Fénelon's integrity, mysticism, anti-rational stance, and individualism. Arguing for Fénelon, Merton is, in fact, arguing for himself. He sees the forces which defeated Fénelon as very much a threat to any person who takes a position opposed to that of the practical men of politics and of the Church.

- "Shakers." Autograph manuscript notes, 2 p. [1963].

After a visit in 1959 to Pleasant Hill, the Shaker town, Merton began a continuing study of the Shakers as a religious and artistic phenomenon. Clearly attracted by the stark beauty of their craftsmanship, Merton also admired their spiritual devotion to God in a kind of "inspired eschatology." Indeed, Merton saw something of Blake in the Shaker devotion to truth as expressed in a maxim such as "Every force evolves a form." In 1964 Merton wrote an article based on these notes for Edward Rice's magazine, *Jubilee,* and in 1966 he wrote the foreword to a book on Shaker furniture by Edward Deming.

- "La Vida Politica." Series of eight calligraphic pen and ink drawings [ca. 1964].

    Encouraged by the artist and calligrapher Ulfert Wilke, Merton began doing calligraphic drawings in 1964. Merton hoped to sell his drawings and use the proceeds to establish a scholarship in memory of James Chaney at Catherine Spalding College. When his drawings went on tour in 1965, Merton wrote some notes in which he explains that the viewer should not become frustrated trying to understand "something that is doubtless not intended to be understood."

- "The Church is Christ Living in the World Today." Typewritten manuscript, with autograph corrections, 2 p. [1964].

    Cardinal Spellman, through Monsignor McCormack, told Merton to revise his script for the film to be shown in the Vatican Pavilion at the New York World's Fair in 1964. Instead of focusing on issues of peace and social justice, Merton was required to write an apologetic piece on the Catholic church as the one true Church. It troubled Merton greatly to revise his work in such a way, but he followed instructions. Shown is a revised second draft of the script in which peace and social justice are still the focal points.

- "Memorandum on Monastic Renewal." Typewritten manuscript (carbon), with autograph corrections and additions, 6 p. 1964.

    Merton warns against taking as a norm monastic communities which are active rather than contemplative. Central to his concern is his fidelity to the spirit of solitude and the life of prayer. Undoubtedly his experience of the growth of mechanization and commercial activity at Gethsemani colored his thoughts on this subject. As Merton says, "The Abbot is a spiritual Father and not merely an administrator," a clear criticism of Dom James.

- *Seeds of Destruction*. New York: Farrar, Straus and Giroux, 1964.

    Inscribed to Victor and Carolyn Hammer. Merton's call for Christians to act against violence, racism, and all forms of social injustice made his a strong voice in the 1960s. The concept of the guilty bystander is central to Merton's writings on society. To think and not act is a betrayal of truth. What made Ghandi so important to Merton was his capacity to remain faithful to truth and service regardless of short-term goals and strategy. This book is a collection of essays and letters divided into three sections: "Black Revolution," "The Diaspora," and "Letters in a Time of Crisis."

- "Letters to a White Liberal." Typewritten manuscript, with autograph corrections, 4 p. [1963].

    This attack on the liberal attitude towards blacks and their struggle for social justice and equality is unflinching in its tone of anger and contempt. Merton felt that race warfare was imminent in America. The passage of the Civil Rights Bill was seen by him as only a start towards beginning real social change; however, Merton felt that white society was fundamentally unwilling to accept blacks as equals. True social change, Merton says, calls for the acceptance by whites of a new social order, which itself will be the result of a peaceful revolution in thinking and attitudes. The lip service paid to equality by white liberals angered Merton because he could see that it would lead only to violence.

The Hermitage Years: 1965–1968

From 1960 Merton was allowed to use the abbey's retreat house as a place of solitude, and on August 17, 1965, the private council met and approved Merton's retirement to the hermitage. These final years of isolation produced new artistic and spiritual growth. Early in 1968 Merton visited California and New Mexico (this journey is recorded in *Woods, Shore, Desert*). Later he was given permission to take an extended leave in order to attend a conference of Benedictine abbots in Bangkok, and to look for possible sites for a hermitage, as well as visit various spiritual leaders in Asia. Merton's death in Bangkok was yet another trauma in a year which had seen the assassination of Martin Luther King, Jr., and Robert Kennedy. Indeed, he died on the same day as the Swiss Protestant theologian Karl Barth (whom many consider the outstanding Christian theologian of the twentieth century) died at his home in Basel. As Mark Van Doren writes in Merton's obituary: "I for one have never known a mind more brilliant, more beautiful, more serious, more playful. . . . His death was more than a blow; it was heartbreaking."

- *The Way of Chuang Tzu.* New York: New Directions, 1965.
  Working from existing translations, Merton assembled this collection of his own "readings" of writings by and about the ancient Taoist writer Chuang Tzu. As he says, "I have enjoyed writing this book more than any other I can remember." Merton considered Chuang Tzu "my own kind of person," enjoying his "direct existential grasp of reality." Merton abhorred the "aggressivity, the ambition, the push, and the self-importance which one must display in order to get along in society."
  Gift of Robert M. Shepherd

- *Seasons of Celebration.* New York: Farrar, Straus and Giroux, 1965.
  The implications of liturgical renewal adopted by Vatican II is the subject of this collection of essays centered on the cycle of the liturgical year. Some of the essays date from the fifties, so Merton draws the attention of the reader to three which he considers most representative of his current thinking: "The Liturgy and Spiritual Personalism," "Easter: The New Life," and "The Good Samaritan." As usual, Merton does not seek "safe and conventional piety."
  Gift of Robert M. Shepherd

- John Howard Griffin. Photograph of Merton's hermitage [1965].

- John Howard Griffin. Portrait photograph of Merton [ca. 1965].

Photograph by John Howard Griffin of Merton's hermitage at Gethsemani, 1965.

■ "The Church in the Contemporary World." Typewritten manuscript, with autograph corrections and additions, 57 p. 1965.

This quickly written and heavily revised essay on the role of the Church in the contemporary, post-Vatican II world is a good example of Merton writing without sufficient forethought. Merton touches on a number of contemporary issues in trying to argue for the relevance of the Church in society. Jumping from Dietrich Bonhoeffer to Teilhard de Chardin to St. Anselm and from scientific materialism to existential atheism, Merton attempts to define the role of the Church. Yet, the final message from this piece is Merton's warning against the growth of military power through applied science, and an appeal to all Christians to value and respect the humanity of all men.

■ *Raids on the Unspeakable.* New York: New Directions, 1966.

In his tongue-in-cheek prologue, Merton gives a few words of advice to his book, one of his favorites, as it enters the world. He asks his book to beware lest its author, "your old man, be called a gnostic anarchist on top of everything else." "Poetry and irony" become the means of confronting the "challenge of the hour, that of dehumanization." The "Unspeakable" is defined as the void which infects all public language and pronouncements, allowing men like Eichmann to draw the "punctilious exactitude of obedience." To be human, to endure, and to triumph with the help of God is the word of this volume, this "little fellow" as Merton calls it.

■ Photographs by Merton of a tree stump [1964].

Merton was fascinated by the stark violence which seemed to spring from this dead root. Such a shape appears on the cover of his book *Raids on the Unspeakable.*

- Photograph of Merton standing by a rhubarb patch [ca. 1966].

- "Feast Day Card" [ca. 1966].

    The above card demonstrates that the monks of Gethsemani have a healthy sense of humor.

- *Conjectures of a Guilty Bystander.* New York: Doubleday, 1966.

    This collection of comments on everything from a dead whale with ulcers being washed ashore near San Francisco to an interpretation of Karl Barth's dream of Mozart — "Fear not, Karl Barth!...Christ remains a child in you. Your books (and mine) matter less than we might think" — ranks as one of Merton's most ironic, funny, and lively books. As he matured as a writer, Merton grew in self-understanding to a quite remarkable degree; this awareness allowed him a greater empathy with his fellow man. He speaks with a voice that compels us to confront our illusions and accept the burden of freedom. We read of a man who is unafraid to admit his humanity and love of others, thereby allowing us to take comfort in both the trials and joy of being human.

    Gift of Robert M. Shepherd

- Thomas Merton. Photograph of Jacques Maritain [1966].

- John Howard Griffin. Photograph of John Howard Griffin, Merton, and Jacques Maritain *(front row, seated left to right)*; *(standing left to right)* Jack Ford, Elizabeth Manuel, Father J. Stanley Murphy, C.S.B., and Daniel Walsh [October 1966].

    On the occasion of Jacques Maritain's final visit to the United States, John Howard Griffin brought him to visit Merton. Merton took the group back to his hermitage to have coffee, listen to music, and read them some of his poems. Later he said mass in Latin for Maritain in the external chapel, and in the evening Maritain spoke to the gathered monks.

- John Howard Griffin. Photograph of Merton giving communion to Jacques Maritain [October 7, 1966].

- "Solitary Life in the Shadow of a Cistercian Monastery." Typewritten manuscript, with autograph corrections, 9 p. October 1966.

    After twenty-five years at Gethsemani, and a little over a year living as a hermit, Merton explains his "exceptional" situation. Before giving a simple description of his eremitic life, Merton states four "basic principles" on the role of the hermit within a cenobitic community. Merton seeks to show that his is not a total aberration of the Rule of Saint Benedict. Indeed, with characteristic humor, he says that he will have to go to the monastery on a regular basis: "Having tried my hand at cooking, I think I will not risk ruining my stomach by eating food which I have myself prepared but will continue to take dinner in the community."

- "D. T. Suzuki: the Man and His Work." Typewritten manuscript, with autograph corrections and additions, 8 p. [1967].

In this lucid essay, Merton explains how the person and thought of Daisetz Suzuki influenced his life and enabled him to gain insight into the various spiritual links between the Western mystical tradition and Zen. Merton met Suzuki on two occasions. One meeting resulted in the publication in *New Directions 17* of one of their dialogues, "Wisdom in Emptiness."

- "A Prayer from the 'De Anima' of Cassiodorus." Typewritten manuscript, with autograph corrections, 5 p. [1967].

- *A Prayer of Cassiodorus.* Worcester: Stanbrook Abbey Press, 1967. Limited edition.

    This sixth-century prayer of the founder of the monastery of Vivarium and former Roman statesman, Magnus Aurelius Cassiodorus, attracted Merton by its "sobriety and light." Very much a classicist, Merton enjoyed the poise, moral seriousness, and beauty of classical writing.

- *Mystics and Zen Masters.* New York: Farrar, Straus and Giroux, 1967.

    The study of Zen was something which Merton found fascinating, and of great value to his understanding of all mystical experience. In his search for enlightenment through a perfect union with God, Merton used Zen as an approach to mystical insight through a discipline of mind. Knowing the great difficulty of trying to explain or analyze Zen, Merton, nonetheless, supplies us with his own thought on what Zen is and what it teaches. The idea of a resolution of all opposites within the void of pure being attracted Merton as did the strict, non-rationalizing approach taken by Zen masters.

    Gift of Robert M. Shepherd

- "Day of a Stranger." Typewritten manuscript (mimeographed), 10 p. 1967.

    In response to a request by a South American editor to describe a "typical day" in his life, Merton wrote this brief article. Merton's ability to see details of his environment afresh is evident throughout. In a matter-of-fact manner he muses with himself and with the reader, raising questions about the structure of life and the meaning of any particular event or action. Living as a well-known hermit, Merton admits, gives to his life an aura of mystical charm that is illusory. However, people insist on thinking that he has a "special message," when, in fact, he is simply a man trying to live his life with some degree of honesty and meaning in a world filled with "blood, lies, fire, hate, the opening of the grave, void."

- Photograph of Merton and Sister Thérèse Lentfoehr [1967].

    At a picnic with his friends the O'Callaghans, Merton mischievously had Sister Thérèse put on a red wool poncho that Tommie O'Callaghan had bought.

- "Graph of My Work." Autograph manuscript (photocopy), 1 p. [1967].

    Merton drew this graph evaluating his books not in terms of sales but rather artistically and spiritually. As can be seen, he was very pleased with at least half of the books listed, with no one book considered the best.

- *Monks Pond.* Nos. 1-4, 1968. Trappist, Kentucky.

   "The purpose of this magazine is to publish a few issues devoted to poetry and to some unusual prose and then go out of business," writes Merton in his introduction to the first volume. A few months later the final number appeared. "So the pond has frozen over — as planned. There was enough material for six issues but it got crammed into four. The problem of losing good poems, of failing to answer letters, of forgetting to send copies, of not notifying poets for months that they had been accepted: all this is the hell of editors. But it was a good experience."

   Gift of Robert M. Shepherd

- "Slowly, slowly." Typewritten manuscript, with autograph corrections, 1 p. 1967.

   One of Merton's most outstanding poems, this hymn stands as the center of *Cables to the Ace.* The tone of reassurance, the simplicity of the lines, and the grace of the language give it a dignity, heightened by its contrast with many of the other poems in the volume.

- *Cables to the Ace.* New York: New Directions, 1968.

   Anticipating the surprise of his readers encountering these experimental poems, Merton informs them that he "has changed his address and his poetics are on vacation." Influenced by the anti-poetry of Nicanor Parra, Merton skillfully plays with tone, balance, form, and meaning in order to explore ways to truth. There are eighty-eight "poems" in the volume, which concludes with the playful phrase, "Pourrait être continué."

   Gift of Robert M. Shepherd

- Photograph of Merton in a study at Gethsemani [ca. 1968].

- Typewritten letter signed, to Mark Van Doren, 1 p. Trappist, Kentucky, July 23, 1968.

   This is the last letter Merton wrote to Mark Van Doren. Full of delight at the prospect of his trip to Asia, Merton writes: "Think of all the cablegrams saying 'RETURN AT ONCE' being shot to Bali, Tibet, Kamchatka, Ceylon, the Maldives, the Endives, the Southern Chives, the Lesser Maundies, the Nether Freeways, the Outer Salvages." In a playful mood, Merton jests that the monastery may have a problem getting him to return. Part of this play may be due to the fact that Robert Lax had visited him in June, bringing with him "innumerable cans of tuna fish and several pints of whiskey, the latter being more practical than the former."

- Philip Stark. Photograph of Merton with his secretary, Brother Patrick Hart, and confrere, Brother Maurice Flood, September 9, 1968.

   This photograph was taken at Merton's hermitage on the day before Merton left Gethsemani for his trip to Asia.

- Photograph of Merton and the Dalai Lama, November 4, 1968.

   In *Merton, By Those Who Knew Him Best,* the Dalai Lama recalls his meeting with Merton: "He made a great impression on me. When I think or feel something Chris-

Merton and the Dalai Lama, 1968.

tian, immediately his picture, his vision, his face comes to me. To the present day. Very nice."

■ Photograph of Merton with fellow members attending the Bangkok conference, December 10, 1968.

■ Photograph of Merton at the Bangkok conference delivering his final lecture, December 10, 1968.

■ Mark Van Doren. Autograph letter (draft), to Dom Flavian, the Abbot of Gethsemani, 1 p. [Connecticut], December 10, 1968.

In this draft reply to the news of Merton's death, Van Doren writes: "He was one of the great persons of our time or of any time. I shall mourn for him as long as I live."

■ Photograph of Merton's funeral mass in Bangkok, December 14, 1968.

The abbot primate of the Bangkok conference, Dom Weakland, celebrated a requiem mass for the repose of Thomas Merton's soul. The vestments worn were white in celebration that Merton was now truly with God.

The Legacy: 1968 – 1988

Merton left many projects incomplete at the time of his death, and his friends and editors have arranged for all important Merton manuscripts to be published. A growing body of scholarship has been added to the steady flow of poetry, essays, and journals which have been published since Merton's death. There have been a number of biographies of Merton (Michael Mott's *The Seven Mountains of Thomas Merton* is the authorized biography), many monographic studies, hundreds of critical articles, and numerous conferences. In all of this activity, there is a distinct danger that Merton is becoming fragmented: there is Merton the poet, the social activist, the mystic, the artist, the rebel, the hermit, the would-be Zen Buddhist, and so on. Merton himself would have found this entertaining. Yet, no matter how varied his interests or how diverse his writings, Merton remains a man of God, his voice clear and his vision constant. His life of prayer and contemplation is an inspiration in its constancy and a challenge in its meaning.

- *Zen and the Birds of Appetite.* New York: New Directions, 1969.

    Merton accepted Zen fully on its own terms. He did not attempt to explain its unspoken way, only to hint at the prospect it offered of spiritual enlightenment through the transcendence of false ego, and, for the Christian, realization of the "manifestation of the Incarnation."

- *Contemplative Prayer.* New York: Herder and Herder, 1969.

    In this last book completed before his death, Merton gives us his mature insights into what it means to exist and to pray. Part of his emphasis is on correcting the impression that prayer is directed away from engagement with the world. For Merton, the life of prayer is a process of constant awakening to the imminence of God in all creation. The troubling aspects of life and history are not simply resolved, nor are they evaded, through prayer and meditation. However, prayer combined with a contemplative orientation results in a spiritual transformation that bears abundant social fruits.
    Gift of Robert M. Shepherd

- *The Geography of Lograire.* New York: New Directions, 1969.

    In the summer of 1968, shortly before he set out on his Asian journey, Merton sent James Laughlin the typescript of a work in progress which Merton projected would run to considerable length. However, he thought that the first book could stand alone.

An exploration of myth, dream, and social anthropology, this ambitious poem is the culmination of a life of reading and contemplation. Essentially a confrontation with the various delusions at the heart of Western civilization, the poem is structured in four cantos: "South," "North," "East," and "West." Hope is seen as residing in the West and East, hell in the North (interestingly, "The most personally subjective part of the long meditation [is] on Eros and Thanos, centering in the New York City Borough of Queens, in the 'North' canto").
Gift of Robert M. Shepherd

■ *Contemplation in a World of Action.* New York: Doubleday, 1971.

Allowing his sense of fun full range, Merton lampoons his public image: "I have myself become a sort of stereotype of the world-denying contemplative — the man who spurned New York, spat on Chicago, and tromped on Louisville, heading for the woods with Thoreau in one pocket, John of the Cross in another, and holding the Bible open at the Apocalypse." Merton's love of the world and concern for monastic renewal combine in this book, in which he argues for the need of contemplation within the modern social context.

■ *The Asian Journal of Thomas Merton.* New York: New Directions, 1973.

This volume contains the edited text of three journals kept by Merton on his 1968 trip to Asia, as well as the text of lectures he delivered during the trip. Merton hoped to learn from contact with Buddhist monasticism, and bring back to the West something of lasting value. The *Journal* teems with observations on life, which range from the most profound to the everyday, and which embody the honest spirit and love of life that informed everything Merton did. Perhaps his deepest spiritual experience took place on December 2, when he approached the three gigantic stone statues of Buddha in Polonnaruwa: "I don't know when in my life I have had such a sense of beauty and spiritual validity running together in one aesthetic illumination... I mean, I know and have seen what I was obscurely looking for." Seven days later Merton died.

■ *Ishi Means Man.* Greensboro: Unicorn Press, 1976.

Inspired by Doris Dana's story of the last survivor of a tribe of California Yana Indians, who died without revealing his name, Merton gathered more material on Indian culture. In this collection of essays and reviews, Merton attempts to reveal a part of the Yana's dignity and expose the cultural genocide they suffered at the hands of the European settlers. Merton also repudiates certain of our cultural myths responsible for our subjugation of other cultures.
Frederic Bancroft Fund

■ Thomas Merton and Robert Lax. *A Catch of Anti-Letters.* Kansas City: Sheed, Andrews and McMeel, 1978.

The friendship of Robert Lax was an immensely meaningful one for Merton. He first met Lax in Mark Van Doren's class on Shakespeare at Columbia. Their shared sense

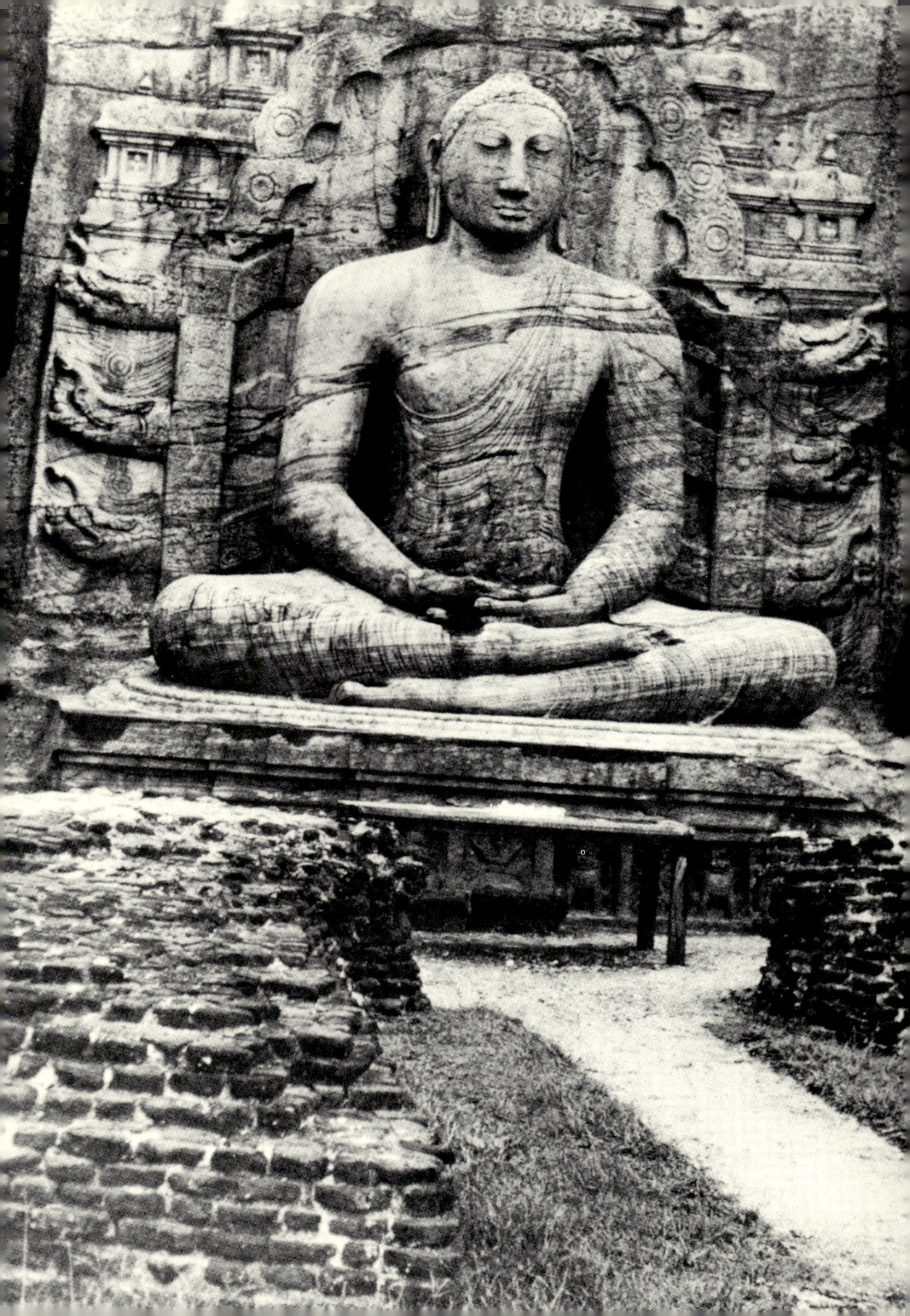

of humor, commitment to art, and social concerns made them fast friends. This collection of letters, covering the years 1962–1967, shows their Joycean use of language (dating from their work on the Columbia *Jester* in 1937) and ease in each other's company. Although they did not see each other very often after leaving Columbia, they retained a comfortable spontaneity in their correspondence which testifies to their instinctive understanding of each other both as artists and men.

Gift of Robert Lax

Eighteen Poems. New York: New Directions, 1985.

These lyric poems are the product of a period of severe spiritual and emotional crisis for Merton. In 1966, while undergoing treatment for a back injury at a hospital in Lexington, Merton met and fell in love with a student nurse. The experience of being in love was both exhilarating and frustrating. These lyrics express Merton's sense of union with all humanity through love and suffering, beauty and joy.

The Alaskan Journal of Thomas Merton. Isla Vista, California: Turkey Press, 1988. One of 140 copies.

En route to Asia in 1968, Merton visited Alaska to scout for possible sites for a new hermitage. As always he wrote daily in a journal, recording thoughts, impressions, and experiences. This journal covers the period from June 7 to October 8. The editor, Robert E. Daggy, decided to simply transcribe Merton's working notebook, giving this journal a spontaneity characteristic of Merton himself. The slipcase has a relief print of a photograph of Alaska taken by Merton.

A Vow of Conversation. New York: Farrar, Straus and Giroux, 1988.

Although the journals for the last twelve years of Merton's life have been placed under restriction, these journals from 1964–1965 have been published because Merton himself did the editing. Covering the period up to the final approval of his request to live as a hermit, the entries are frank, often funny, and always honest. His account of his secret trip to New York to meet with Daisetz Suzuki, his thoughts on his abbot Dom James Fox, his visitors, his studies, all make for compelling reading. The final entries are from the hermitage, where Merton confronts the implications of the solitary life: "The five days I have had in real solitude have been a revelation, and whatever questions I may have had about it before are now answered. . . . Everything about this life is rewarding."

Gift of Robert Giroux

Photograph by Merton of a statue of Buddha in Polonnaruwa, 1968.

Index

"Abelard," 35
Abelard, Peter, 35
Alaskan Journal of Thomas Merton, The, 59
Alpha Delta Phi fraternity, 13, 14
"Angel of the Annunciation" (drawing), 16, 17
Antonucci, Emil, 44, 45
Anvil Press, 21
Apollinaire, Guillaume, 21
"April," 22
Aristotle, 16, 21
"Army Conversation" (drawing), 16
"Art and Worship," 38
Ascent to Truth, The, 29
Asian Journal of Thomas Merton, The, 57
Auden, W. H. (Wystan Hugh), 21

Bancroft, Frederic, 36, 57
Barth, Karl, 50, 52
Behavior of Titans, The, 42
Benedictines, 34, 35, 37, 41
Bennett, Tom, 9
Bermuda, 13
"Black Revolution," 48
Blake, William, 14, 47
Bloy, Leon, 29
Bonhoeffer, Dietrich, 51
Bread in the Wilderness, 31
Buddha, 57, 58
Buridan, Jean, 16

Cables to the Ace, 54
Camaldolese, 28, 35, 41
"Cana," 20
"Candlemas Procession, The," 21
Carthusians, 28, 35, 41
Cassiodorus, Magnus Aurelius, 53
Catch of Anti-Letters, A, 57
Catherine Spalding College, 48
"Catholic Hour, The," 35
Catholic Worker, 44
Cézanne, Paul, 13

Chaney, James, 48
"Chant to Be Used in Processions Around a Site with Furnaces," 47
Chardin, Teilhard de, 51
Chesed, 47
"Christian Ethics and Nuclear War," 42
Chuang Tzu, 50
"Church in the Contemporary World, The," 51
"Church is Christ Living in the World Today, The," 48
Cistercian Contemplatives, 22
Cistercian Order of the Strict Observance, 9, 18, 26, 28, 33, 34, 35, 41, 42
Clement of Alexander, 46
Columbia University Yearbook, 7, 13, 14
Columbian, The, 14
Conjectures of a Guilty Bystander, 52
Constitution on the Liturgy, 38
Contemplation in a World of Action, 57
Contemplative Prayer, 56
Curtis Brown Ltd., 8

"D. T. Suzuki: the Man and His Work," 52
Daggy, Robert E., 59
"Daily Schedule," 20
Dalai Lama, 54, 55
"Dans le Desert de Dieu," 34
"Dawn. The Hour of Lauds," 46
"Day of a Stranger," 53
de Toledano, Ralph, 14, 15
Deming, Edward, 47
Devot Christ, Perpignan, France, 31
"Diaspora, The," 48
Disputed Questions, 39, 41, 42
Doubleday, 52, 57
"Drunk Danse" (drawing), 16

Early Poems/1940–42, 21
"Easter: The New Life," 50
Eighteen Poems, 59
Elected Silence see *Seven Storey Mountain, The*
"Elegy for the Monastery Barn," 33
Eliot, T. S. (Thomas Stearns), 21, 22, 23
Emblems of a Season of Fury, 47

Fadiman, Clifton, 25
Farrar & Rinehart, 16
Farrar, Straus & Cudahy, 35, 37, 38, 41
Farrar, Straus and Giroux, 48, 50, 53, 59
"Feast Day Card," 52
Fénelon, Francois, 47
Figures for an Apocalypse, 23, 29
Finnegans Wake, 15
Flood, Brother Maurice, 54
"Footrace, The" (drawing), 16
"For My Brother: Reported Missing in Action, 1943," 23
Ford, Jack, 52
Fox, Dom James, 48, 59
Franciscans, 13, 16
Freedgood, Seymour, 13
"From the Legend of St. Clement," 29
Fulbert, Canon of Notre-Dame, 35

Gandhi, Mohandas Karamchand, 48
Geography of Lograire, The, 56
Gerdy, Robert, 13
Gethsemani, Abbey of Our Lady of, 7, 9, 13, 18, 20, 21, 22, 25, 26, 31, 36, 37, 42, 43
Gethsemani Magnificat, 26
Gibney, Robert, 13
Giroux, Robert, 7, 25, 59

— *61* —

"Good Samaritan, The," 46, 50
"Grace's House," 47
"Graph of My Work," 53
Green, Graham, 25
Griffin, John Howard, 50, 51, 52

Habich, William, 31
Hagia Sophia, 46, 49
Hammer, Caroline, 37, 48
Hammer, Victor, 7, 37, 41, 42, 46, 48
Harcourt, Brace & Company, 9, 25, 28, 29, 31, 33, 35
Harcourt, Brace & World, 46
Harriet Monroe Memorial Prize, 29
Hart, Brother Patrick, 54
Harwood, Del, 23
Heloise, 35
Herder and Herder, 56
"High Morning. The Hour of Tierce," 46
Hindemith, Paul, 35
Hiroshima, 44
Hopkins, Gerard Manley, 28
"How Long We Wait," 20
Huxley, Aldous, 39
"Hymn, of Not Much Praise for New York City," 22

Ishi Means Man, 57

Jester, 7, 13, 14, 16, 59
"Journal of My Escape from the Nazis, The" *see My Argument with the Gestapo*
Joyce, James, 15, 59
Jubilee, 40, 41, 47

Kacmarcik, Frank, 37
Kafka, Franz, 18
Kellogg, Helen Hall, 26
Kennedy, Robert, 50
King, Martin Luther, Jr., 50
Kirk, Grayson, 7

"Labyrinth, The," 14
Ladder of Paradise, 29
Last of the Fathers, The, 33
Laughlin, James, 23, 36, 56

Lax, Robert, 7, 8, 13, 14, 15, 16, 22, 54, 57, 59
Lentfoehr, Thérèse, 7, 20, 21, 22, 25, 28, 29, 31, 34, 37, 42, 53
"Let the Poor Man Speak," 41
"Letter of Fulbert of Chartres to King Robert," 47
"Letter to My Friends," 18, 20
"Letters to a White Liberal," 48
"Life at Gethsemani," 34
"Liturgy and Spiritual Personalism, The," 41, 50
Louisville Courier-Journal, 31
Luce, Clare Boothe, 25

Man in the Divided Sea, A, 20, 22
Manuel, Elizabeth, 52
Marcks, Gerhard, 36
Maritain, Jacques, 52
Mazzolari, Don Primo, 41
McCormack, Monsignor, 48
Melleray, Abbey of Our Lady of, 26
"Memorandum on Monastic Renewal," 48
Meng Tzu, 42
Merton, By Those Who Knew Him Best, 54
Merton, John Paul, 13, 21, 22
Merton, Owen, 9, 13
Merton, Ruth, 9, 13
Merton, Thomas
  Alaska, 59
  Bangkok, 9, 50, 55
  Baptism as Roman Catholic, 13
  California, 56
  Cambridge, 9
  Columbia College, 7, 9, 14
  Columbia University, 7
  Conscientious objector, 18
  Consecration as monk, 20
  Death, 55
  Drawings by, 16, 17, 29, 30, 31, 48
  Greenwich Village, 14
  Hermitage, 50, 51, 54
  Lectures and sermons, 31, 34, 38

  Master of novices, 28, 33, 34
  Master of scholastics, 28, 29
  New Mexico, 50
  Notebooks and journals, 16, 20, 21, 31
  Olean, New York, 14, 15, 16
  Ordination as priest, 26, 27
  Photographs by, 42, 51, 52, 58, 59
  Photographs of, 2, 13, 14, 15, 18, 20, 25, 26, 27, 33, 34, 36, 43, 44, 50, 52, 53, 54, 55
  Polonnaruwa, Ceylon, 57
  Radio broadcasts, 35
  St. Bonaventure, 16, 18
  University Medal for Excellence, 7, 44
  Zen garden, 42
Migne, Jacques Paul, 38
Monks Pond, 54
Monroe, Harriet, 29
Morison, Stanley, 37
Mott, Michael, 33, 56
"Mount Athos," 40
Mozart, Wolfgang Amadeus, 52
Murphy, J. Stanley, 52
My Argument with the Gestapo, 17, 18, 19
"My Reasons for Asking Exemption from Combat Duty," 18
Mystics and Zen Masters, 53

Nativity Kerygma, 37
"Nature and Art in William Blake," 14
New Directions, 22, 23, 26, 29, 31, 35, 38, 42, 44, 46, 47, 50, 51, 53, 54, 56, 57, 59
New Seeds of Contemplation, 44
New York World's Fair, 48
"'News I Read as a Secular, The,'" 37
"Night Before the Battle, The," 14, 15
No Man Is an Island, 34, 35
"Notes for a Philosophy of Solitude," 42

"Notes on the Benedictine Rule," 37
"Notes on Sacred Art," 34
"Novitiate Journal," 20

O'Callaghan, Tommie (Mrs. Frank), 53
"The Ointment," 21
Original Child Bomb, 44, 45
Ox Mountain Parable of Meng Tzu, The, 7, 42

Parola ai Poveri, La, 41
Parrar, Nicanor, 54
Parrhesia, 41
"Pasternak Affair, The," 39
Pasternak, Boris, 39
Pasternak-Merton: Six Letters, 1958–1960, 40
"Patriotic Singer" (drawing), 16
Peele, George, 21
Picard, Max, 36
Pius XII, 33
"Poetry and Contemplation: a Reappraisal," 37
"Poetry and the Contemplative Life," 23
"Prayer," 36
"Prayer from the *De Anima* of Cassiodorus, A," 53
Prayer of Cassiodorus, A, 53
"Prisoner's Base," 25
Prometheus: A Meditation, 37, 39

Raids on the Unspeakable, 51
Random House, 8
"Red or Dead," 47
"Reflections on the Character and Genius of Fénelon," 47
"A Responsory. (for Paul Hindemith)," 35
Rice, Edward, 13, 14, 15, 26, 47
Rilke, Rainer Maria, 21
Rule of St. Benedict, 52

Saffron, Morris H., 34
St. Anselm, 51
St. Antonin, France, 14
St. Augustine, 21
St. Bernard, 33, 35
St. Bonaventure College, 16, 18, 37

St. John Climacus, 29
St. John of the Cross, 21, 26, 29, 57
"St. John of the Ladder," 29
St. Lutgarde, 29
"St. Malachy," 29
St. Matthew, 31
"St. Paul," 20
St. Teresa of Avila, 26
St. Thomas Aquinas, 29
St. Thomas the Apostle, 26
"Saints Peter and Paul," 31
Saturday Review, 31
Seasons of Celebration, 50
Second Vatican Council, 38, 39, 50
Secular Journal of Thomas Merton, 13, 37, 38
Seeds of Contemplation, 25, 26, 35
Seeds of Destruction, 48
"Sentences" *see No Man Is an Island*
Seven Mountains of Thomas Merton, The, 56
Seven Storey Mountain, The, 7, 9, 13, 20, 24, 25, 28, 31
"Shakers," 47
Sheed, Andrews and McMeel, 57
Sheehy, Eugene P., 29
Sheen, Fulton J., 25
Shepherd, Robert M., 8, 25, 29, 35, 41, 46, 50, 52, 53, 54, 56, 57
Sign of Jonas, The, 31, 32
"A Signed Confession of Crimes Against the State," 16
Silent Life, The, 35
"Slowly, slowly," 54
Solitary Life, The, 40, 41
"Solitary Life in the Shadow of a Cistercian Monastery," 52
Somoza, Luis A., 39
Spellman, Cardinal Francis, 48
Spirit of Simplicity, The, 25
Stamperia del Santuccio, 7, 38, 40, 41, 42, 46
Stanbrook Abbey Press, 53
Stark, Philip, 54
"Straits of Dover, The," 14
Strange Islands, The, 33, 35

Suzuki, Daisetz T., 52, 59

Tears of the Blind Lions, The, 29
Temoignages, 34
"Texts from Saint Bernard," 29
"Things in their Identity," 26
Thirty Poems, 20, 22
Thomas Merton on Peace, 44
Thomas Merton Reader, A, 46
Thomas of Cantimpre, 29
Thoreau, Henry David, 57
"Thoughts in Solitude," 36
Tower of Babel, The, 35, 36
"Trappists Working," 20
Trilling, Diana, 22
Turkey Press, 59

Ulmann, Albert, 21
Unicorn Press, 57

Van Doren, Mark, 7, 9, 13, 15, 16, 18, 20, 22, 23, 26, 31, 34, 36, 44, 50, 54, 55, 57
Verba Seniorum, 38
"Vida Politica, La" (drawings), 48
"Viewpoints" *see No Man Is an Island*
Vow of Conversation, A, 59

Walsh, Daniel, 13, 52
Waters of Siloe, 28
Waugh, Evelyn, 25, 28, 31
Way of Chuang Tzu, The, 50
Weakland, Dom, 55
"Whale and the Ivy, The" *see Sign of Jonas, The*
What Are these Wounds?, 29
What Is Contemplation?, 25
What Ought I to Do?, 38
"What Shall I Do?", 38
"What to Do if It Rains Blood," 47
Wilke, Ulfert, 48
"Wisdom in Emptiness," 53
Wisdom of the Desert Fathers, 38
Woods, Shore, Desert, 50
World of Silence, 36

Zen and the Birds of Appetite, 56
Zen Buddhism, 39, 42, 53, 56

Fifteen hundred copies printed
Produced by Columbia University's Office of Publications
Designed by Marjorie Coyne
Edited by Kevin Clift
Composed by Gutenberg Printing
Printed by Mered Printing Services